What's Right with You:
An Interactive Character
Development Guide

D0874775

To Mickey,

What's Right with You:
An Interactive Character
Development Guide

Marjorie S. Schiering

Marjorie S. Schiering

ROWMAN & LITTLEFIELD
INTERNATIONAL

London • New York

Published by Rowman & Littlefield
A wholly owned subsidiary of The Rowman & Littlefield Publishing Group, Inc.
4501 Forbes Boulevard, Suite 200, Lanham, Maryland 20706
www.rowman.com

Unit A, Whitacre Mews, 26-34 Stannary Street, London SE11 4AB

British Library Cataloguing-in-Publication Information Available

Library of Congress Cataloging-in-Publication Data Available

978-1-4758-2683-8 (cloth : alk. paper)
978-1-4758-2684-5 (pbk. : alk. paper)
978-1-4758-2685-2 (electronic)

∞™ The paper used in this publication meets the minimum requirements of American National Standard for Information Sciences—Permanence of Paper for Printed Library Materials, ANSI/NISO Z39.48–1992.

Printed in the United States of America

Contents

Foreword

In the years that I have known and worked with Dr. Marjorie Schiering at Molloy College, I have witnessed not only a clever, creative educator but also a caring professor, a deeply spiritual woman whose concern for others comes from a life committed to her large and loving family and to her ministries to the sick and lonely. That love of and concern for others naturally found its way into her classrooms, many and varied, over the years of her teaching.

From elementary classes in Ohio to the poorest areas of North Carolina to elementary and middle school in New York, then to college settings and now to graduate sessions at Molloy on Long Island, she always focused on the individual, on the student's needs, and on approaches that made the student comfortable and ready to learn. In brief, she developed an awareness of the student as a person with a heart as well as a head, a person deserving respect, understanding, and love.

This text tells the story of her journey to her interest in and study of character development, of the theory and application of techniques for creating the best possible atmosphere for successful teaching. Section One conveys the value and nature of the care a good teacher brings to students, the traits of an educator best able to mold the minds of students, but from there, Dr. Schiering moves to the practical, offering games and tools to relax the student and make him or her comfortable and receptive to lessons and ready to learn.

Her detailed instructions have been tested and honed throughout her fifty years of elementary, middle school, and college teaching. These shared experiences give the reader the method she so satisfactorily employs. She shows us educators how and why we need to care. And she draws on not only her own rich experience but also the experience of her sons and colleagues, some of whom have contributed some chapters to the book. True stories of how genuine concern for the student's struggles brought success to those employing that concern make concrete the points she makes. Some stories touch the heart; others make one laugh. All make one think.

Oscar Hammerstein, lyricist for Richard Rodgers, composed a sad, frightening poem for the musical *South Pacific*, in 1949; the song began like this: "You've got to be taught to hate and fear." He offered a reflection on how bigotry begins. But no! Dr. Schiering travels a better road as she addresses her fellow educators. She tells them thus: "You've got to be taught to love and care if you seek to reach the students before you."

Dr. Schiering tells us why and how to do so. And she calls on her years of joyful educating, probing research, prolific lecturing on both sides of the Atlantic, and her own faith and family life to invite us to put down our put-downs and lift up our students. Communicate kindness, she says, for kindness communicates.

Robert Kinpoitner, PhD
Chair, Royal English Department
Molloy College

Additional Foreword

Character counts. It certainly counted in the past when questions of what it meant to be a good person were regarded as central to the education of young people, and it counts just as much today. In fact, character education may never have been quite as important as it is presently in American society.

For one thing, we are living through a period in which faith in those social institutions that once provided moral guidance has been strongly eroded. According to the results of a 2016 Gallup Poll, only 20 percent of Americans had a great deal of trust in churches and religious organizations. An even smaller number had a great deal of faith in the Office of the Presidency (16%), the U.S. Supreme Court (15%), public schools (14%), and the criminal justice system (9%). Congress, which at one time was held in such high regard that President John F. Kennedy could write a book entitled *Profiles in Courage* about its members, stands at a record low approval with only 3 percent of Americans having much confidence in this essential branch of government.

Another factor that makes character education in our schools so vital is that students themselves seem woefully confused about basic issues of right and wrong. As anyone who has ever taught ethics to elementary, high school, and even college students will tell you, ethical subjectivism—the belief that moral judgments simply express opinions or preferences—reigns supreme among America's youth. When presented with a case involving lying, cheating, stealing, and so forth, the common refrain that one will typically hear from almost all students is something along the lines of "Who am I to say how other people ought to behave?" While the reticence that these students may have to point their finger of moral disapproval at others may be admirable, it also shows the difficulty that many young people have in making moral judgments at all.

Finally, in the past, common standards of character were fairly uniformly presented at home, in schools, and in churches. Of course, this sort of moral cohesiveness undoubtedly led to a kind of crude absolutism and the persecution of those who strayed too far from the moral norms of the culture. Nonetheless, it was certainly far easier for children in particular to navigate their way through the murky waters of moral behavior when the standards for such behavior were clear, somewhat consistent, and fairly uniform. Today, we live in a multicultural society with a panoply of different visions of the good life. Making sense of basic issues of right and wrong is difficult enough for the fairly well-educated adult; it is all but bewildering for most young people.

So, we definitely need character education to be taught in schools and, even more importantly, we need it to be taught the right way in order for it to be effective. This is why I'm so grateful that Dr. Marjorie Schiering has applied her considerable skills as an educational theorist to this question. The present work is not just some abstract exploration of moral theory. It's a hands-on, interactive guide that provides essential tools for character development.

What's Right with You is certainly a useful resource for teachers trying to figure out how to introduce character education in the classroom or for parents seeking to jump-start their own children's moral development. But this is also the kind of text that all of us could profit from reading multiple times. As Dr. Schiering points out in the book's introduction, "you can only give to another that which you have for yourself." If we want the next generations of America's youth to be more tolerant, more accepting, more responsible for their own behavior, then the proper place to start is not with the children in our classrooms or homes but with ourselves.

The world that we inhabit is one that is filled with conflict; inequality; and racial, ethnic, and sexual intolerance. The only way that the world will become a better place is if we become better people. But that will only happen if we as a society begin to recognize the importance of character education and are willing to incorporate the best practices of character development into the classroom. And, as far as I'm concerned, there is no better place to start this process than with the book you are holding in your hands right now.

Michael S. Russo, Ph.D.
Professor of Philosophy and Ethics
Molloy College

Preface

If someone were to ask you to reflect and then write about a couple of things that are important to you, what would you write? For that matter, what are you thinking right now as an answer to that question? Are you thinking any one of these: money, job, car, house, food, clothing, vacation, computer, cell phone, and/or the Internet? Those generic answers have two aspects to them. The first is that each could be considered important at any time of the day, anywhere, and year-round. Second, each one is something materialistic.

Now, let's try this. What do you suppose are at most two important "non-materialistic" things to you or others? Are you thinking any of these: family, significant other, parents, love, caring, talking, being kind, relatives, faith path, respect, and/or friendship? These also are generic answers, and each may be considered important at any time of the day, anywhere, and year-round.

At this paragraph's end there is another question to ponder about what may be of importance to you. The major change in this question is that the *location* is not widespread or across-the-board, as was the case in the previous questions. This new specificity of location makes all the difference in the reflection and answer, because in this instance you are concerned with a narrow expanse and perhaps not just with yourself but also with those around you. "What do you suppose are a few of the most important things in a classroom, at any grade level?"

Having looked at the short lists in the first two paragraphs, you may consider combining parts of them or coming up with something entirely new/ different from those listed. You may think of "students" or the "teacher" as being of utmost importance. Well, those are the two that immediately came to this author's mind as an answer, along with the understanding that we are all teachers and learners, simultaneously.

The purpose of this book is to address what things are most important in a classroom and discover or reinforce the concept that the classroom is a microcosm of the communities in which we live and expands to a much wider population area as well. With that awareness, it is apparent that, first and foremost, the *classroom atmosphere must be conducive to learning*. Character education/teaching and its accompanying character development/growth address what it means to be a person of good character and how to make that meaning possible. The realization and achievement of these things are why this book has been written. What the author hopes is that through the initial incorporation of one life/classroom idea of "No put-downs. . . . Only lift-ups!" the atmosphere of the classroom will be harmonious. The book builds on methods to teach oneself and others ways to be a person of good character.

Overall, the most important aspect of a classroom, workshop, workplace, home, community, or anywhere, is one's feeling good about himself or herself so much so that that environment is a *place of comfort*, a place where modeled behaviors are filled with emphasizing what's right with you and self-assuredness is the mainstay. When that place exists, true learning happens.

For this book, a distinction isn't made by age or grade level about the topics of self-esteem and character development. In addition, no other category, such as gender, socioeconomic status, aptitude, race, religion, or politics, separates one person from another. The pages of this writing have *one* mind-set addressed.

One mind-set: *The singularity of purpose of this book focuses on learning about means to educate not just for the sake of educating or passing a test but also for living civility, as well as good citizenship, through self-acceptance and self-worth. There is a focus on the positives of you and me.*

Subsequently, you are invited to examine the content of this book, to analyze the premises provided, and to use the activities in your classroom or in your daily experiences. For what, you may question? The answer would be for the betterment of the communities we create and in which we already live, whether in the school, workplace, or home.

Acknowledgments

First I recognize a Higher Power that has given me the ability to write and brought the people in this Acknowledgment section into my life. There is my husband, George, who tirelessly devoted his time to photocopying activities, making pdf files, making copies of the manuscript with and without figures and photos, and reading every word of the manuscript many times. Frankly, his steadfast allegiance in my behalf to get the words on the pages has served as a daily source of encouragement. His saying that he loves the way I write inspires me to do so. Overall, he's been my go-to guy.

Beginning teaching in Ohio and then a move to the south would find me acknowledging my fifth-grade students who taught me lifelong lessons about how to survive prejudice, discrimination, bullying, and harassment. Emulating their strength of will, determination, and desire to persevere in times of trouble could and has moved mountains.

I would like to mention the following people as those who, along life's path, led me to this point of writing a book on character education and development. We either presented together or they did the reading of my manuscripts, contributed to this book, and/or offered encouragement.

Dr. Rita Dunn is acknowledged as my mentor in the St. John's University doctorate program. She gave verification of my teaching methodology. Her praising my writing and her constant encouragement shaped my desire to be published. The memories of her from 1995 when we first met and even beyond her passing in 2009 have served as a force of encouragement. She was steadfast as she made arrangements for me to present my classroom teaching techniques at conferences here and in Europe between 1996 and the early 2000s. But, none of this would have been possible if not for Debra Thomas from North Rockland Teacher's Center. She is acknowledged as she insisted that I go for my doctorate, and brought the instructional leadership doctorate program to our Rockland County district.

Angela Sullivan, EdD is recognized for always encouraging me to "stick with it." She was a study and writing partner during our doctorate candidate years, and her organizational skills kept me on track. She has been a friend for at least twenty years, and she wrote chapter 14 in this book.

James Million is appreciated for his sociocentricity commentary and concept of one's self-esteem. He is a source of support and true friendship. Colleagues Rickey Moroney, Francine Wisnewski, and Drs. Laura Shea-Doolan, Rita Taylor Pat Mason, Audra Cerruto, Trish Eckardt, Carrie McDermott, Vicky Giouroukakis, Eve Dieringer, Barbara Hayes, and Anthony Marino are acknowledged for their contributions to books, endorsements of this or previous books, or presentations we did together here and abroad. Molloy's IT persons Ben Sales, Joseph Kuczyk, Dennis Neary, Dave Friedrich, Kevin Cooper, and Kevin Milella are acknowledged for their continual assistance with computer-related endeavors for the character development workshops.

Drew Bogner, Ph.D. the president of Molloy College, is acknowledged for his continual help and work on our coauthored book *Teaching and Learning: A Model for Academic and Social Cognition* (2011). He made valuable suggestions that were used then and now regarding the "voice" of a book and asking of questions within the text to stimulate introspection and conversations among the readers. Then, there's his writing of the foreword for *Teaching Creative and Critical Thinking: An Interactive Workbook* (2016). His character development incentives and the importance of civility have proven to be invaluable at our college.

Marie Calder is acknowledged for her reading the first version of all my manuscripts and offering comments regarding their contents. A dear friend since we worked together many years ago, she is tremendously kind and always available to help. While with us, Allen Rauch, PhD was of the same ilk.

Dr. Madeline Craig is acknowledged for her comments regarding the flow of this book's text and clarity of context. Her attention to such things as test scores versus social literacy, offering divergent Journal and/or Discussion Questions for several chapters, and suggesting further explanation of terms added directness to this book.

Diane Forneri, administrative assistant to the president of Molloy and its board of directors is recognized for her help over several years as well as in the organization of the aforementioned 2011 book. In the process, Diane went on to be a colleague of great value.

Judy Trinder, Louisa Quiambao, and Danielle Albanese-Samuel from Continuing Education have helped arrange Project SAVE workshops since 2000 and Dignity for All Students Act (DASA) since 2013. Their organizing and setting up workshops, collating evaluations, and/or scheduling of workshops are appreciated.

Joshua Schiering, my son, is acknowledged for his contribution to this book with the writing of chapters 10 and 11. His ideas on eradicating bullying and accepting, as well as giving an apology have been used in Molloy College's character development workshops these past four years. Joshua's brother, Seth, is acknowledged for his contributions to this book in speaking to doctoral candidates when he was sixteen years old. And, his sister Mara Moore is acknowledged for her contributions to this book about being responsible.

Robert Kinpoitner, PhD, chairman of the Royal English Department at Molloy College, is acknowledged for his helpfulness, being a person who gives without asking for anything in return, his arranging for me to teach children's literature for the Royal English Department, and also for his being my grammarian on all of the books I've authored. Additionally, he is recognized for his impeccable sense of humor that may diffuse a difficult situation or just be present to bring a smile to one's face and heart. Furthermore, he exemplifies communicating kindness.

Amy Meyers, PhD, read this manuscript and made contributions to this text, as well as met with me numerous times to discuss means for bringing character development to our communities. With a fine sense of humor she demonstrates compassion and caring in her teaching and friendship.

Michael Russo, Ph.D. is acknowledged for his steadfast encouragement concerning my writing, his positivity, and contributions to this book and the 2015 one on Creative Thinking.

Other appreciated contributors of anecdotes, comments, and paragraphs in their field of expertise, or slice-of-life stories in this book and not mentioned previously include Tim Ryley, Majed Hanna, Nora Miller, M. After, Lauren Spotkov, Karla Umanzor, Lou Cino, Marina, Landyn, Katie Schiering, Mara Moore, Alexandra Panzarino, Joan Byrne, Drs. Jonathan Borkum, Joanne O'Brien, Teri Rouse, DASA workshop attendees Nicole DeAngelis, Cecelia Fisher, and Rosalie Rivera-Chacon.

Tom Koerner, PhD, vice president of Rowman and Littlefield's Education Division has helped me since 2010 with respect to giving ideas about writing style and topics, as well as ideas for this book's anecdotal section. He has continually provided guidance and encouragement. His associate editor, Carlie Wall, is also given acknowledgment for assisting me with the last two books. Her continued help with e-mails to answer questions and phone conversations has been of the greatest importance. Carlie has been responsible on numerous occasions for guiding me through the process of publishing. These afore-named individual's dedication to teaching and learning is immense. Production manager Brindha Thirumoorthy and copyeditor Sivakumar Vijayaraghavan's works are also acknowledged with appreciation.

ADDITIONAL ACKNOWLEDGMENTS

As my experiential past affects the present and future, the following persons are also acknowledged for their contributions to my writing with the idea of assisting others along life's paths: my parents Mollie and Red After; friend Daisy Schneider; from my teen years there is, Ms. Carragher, my 10th grade social studies teacher who said, "I believe in you." Next there is our children and their significant others, Matt and Maddy, Alyssha and Paul Miro, Josh and Katie, Jolie, Mara and Dave Moore, Seth and Carolina; my nephew Jonathan Borkum and his sister Debbie Goss, as well as the 3,000+ students who I have taught and from whom I've learned.

SPECIAL ACKNOWLEDGMENT

As in the previous two books, Eileen Chapman is acknowledged with tremendous gratitude for her formatting expertise, transference of text into folders, text structure, and being available for assisting with a variety of other technological components. Her allegiance to this project as well as the others knew no limits. She's a colleague who became a friend and came to know the substance of my works. Thank you, Eileen, doesn't seem to be enough, but will have to do in that you are remarkable in your steadfastness for helping others. You are a teacher in the truest sense, as you have shared with others not just your knowledge but your caring as well.

Introduction

This book is organized in a somewhat unusual way, as it's designed to ask you questions that are planned to stimulate your thinking and, one hopes, bring about sharing with others. You might ask, "Share what?" The answer is sharing what you're thinking about the topic or theme of a particular chapter. You are led to examine your own thinking and feelings while being cognizant of those in others. With these goals in mind, each chapter has a specific objective that focuses either on character education/teaching or its accompanying development/growth. *Most* chapters have an activity that supports the teaching of that chapter. Each activity is delineated by its purposes and a set of directions on how to conduct it. The activities are for practical application of the chapter's content material.

There is attention given to this author's social cognition model. The components of the model are provided and include thinking and feelings intertwined (cognitive collective) influencing our behavior and being reciprocal. Then there are beliefs and values that shape our personalities and reflection, serving as the model's foundation. Social experiences, regardless of their place of origin, are seen as the catalyst for one's conduct.

This book, in part, addresses antisocial behaviors. Topics such as bullying, harassment, discrimination, and prejudice are discussed. The cause of each of these behaviors and possible ways to prevent them are provided. Basically, bringing awareness to the six international traits of a person of good character, and the topics of the chapters are addressed through *interactive learning*, which involves active engagement in the acquisition of presented material.

Other topics in this book include accepting and giving an apology; having a sense of self-worth by recognizing what's "right" with you and me; an intervention program for character enhancement; a look-see at one's experiential past that impacts behaviors; conversing "with" as opposed to "at" or "to" others;

1

getting to know oneself; defining and then having examples of respect, caring, and trustworthiness; being a good citizen, being fair, and being responsible.

A section on decision-making is provided in a graphic organizer format and through role-playing. Stressful situations that impinge on being a person of good character are discussed with causes listed and means to counteract them provided. In total there are five appendices.

The concept of one's "being enough" is given attention along with ways to conduct oneself that promote being the best of oneself on an ongoing and regular basis. A chart on the reciprocity of thinking is addressed, and closing comments include three reflections from a post-character development workshop. Contributions from present-day teachers teaching character development, along with the opinions and ideas of former teachers, student learners, teacher candidates, and others not in the field of education are part of this book. The *activities* in this book were originally created during Schiering's teaching career for the elementary, middle school or college classrooms, as well as character development workshops beginning in 2000. They have been modified between that year and the present year, 2017. Additionally, the workshops have been conducted each month from September through June and most recently have been scheduled for July.

This book emphasizes that you can give to another only that which you have for yourself. This would include respect, caring, being fair, and the other behaviors of a person with good character. The idea is that *before* you have a classroom where academics are addressed, the atmosphere of the setting needs to be one where those in it feel safe, comfortable, and secure.

Therefore, the first and most important things about any classroom addresses the components involved in civility and developing character traits representing concern for oneself and others. While doing or being such may be a lifetime process, this book serves to demonstrate how to have character education and development while practicing their components daily. When doing this "practicing," each one comes to realize that he or she is of value and embraces the ideas of acceptance of self and others.

Overall, contributors' writing and mine, strive to teach this book's subject matter in an engaging and user-friendly manner. This presentation is accomplished by recognizing how each of the book's topics impacts character education and development in the classroom, as well as school, workshops, workplace, and home.

BOOK'S AUDIENCE

This book is for you. It is designed to hold conversations with you and you with yourself and others by asking thought-provoking questions and stimulating your thinking and feeling processes. It is for all those who, at one time or another, have been aware of their feeling self and thinking self as being simultaneous experiences. Sometimes, we have a sense of being different from others and other times have situations where reactions are nearly the same. Regardless, it is the conversations of our lives and the experiences that we have that shape our personalities/character and resultant behaviors. The audience is for those willing to receive and share instruction on how to be involved in character development. It's for persons, regardless of a title that labels them, who want to bring about positive thinking and actions to be modeled.

This book is for changing indifference to caring, dislike to like, self-doubt to self-efficacy and acceptance. And, it's also about daily living that is optimistic and hopeful, filled with enthusiasm even when it seems that such an emotion is impossible or marginalized.

This book is for realizing that in the throes of adversity there is something that can be done to change that to thinking and feeling positivity. It is for all those who believe that one person can make a difference by instituting the six international traits of a person of good character and doing this by demonstrating reliability and being dependable. This book is for those who can change negative self-talk to uplifting self-talk that insures for oneself and others a safe and congenial environment, wherever that may be. This book is for those willing to realize that character development is a process that may take a lifetime to complete. And so, in one way or another, this book is not just for you but for all of us.

AUTHOR'S PHILOSOPHY

The author firmly believes and has practiced her entire teaching career the following:

1. Before any subject matter is taught, there must be classroom community building that results in good feelings about self and others.
2. Every classroom or anywhere "social cognition" occurs there needs to be a place of comfort for learning to occur.
3. How one thinks and feels impacts on what one says and does
4. Everyone is a teacher of something.
5. Whether conducting a workshop or teaching, the assemblage needs to be actively engaged and conversing with one another. This interaction includes the one assigned as the leader.
6. The six international traits of "good" character (respectful, fair, caring, trustworthy, responsible, good citizen) are of utmost importance.

7. There needs to be laughter in ourselves so we can enjoy what we're doing and share that delight.
8. Our "conscious will" determines the type of person modeled for others to emulate by our choosing to be a person of good character.
9. Talking "with" one another as opposed to talking "to" or "at" others is vital as a component of conversation excellence.

Section I

Chapter 1

Character Education/Teaching: Character Development/Growth

Book Notation: The author explains that each chapter in this book *focuses* on classroom instruction regarding character education and character development between grades one and sixteen-plus. However, the book's chapters, addressing means for teaching these two programs, also apply to each individual reading this book, as we are all teachers in the home or in occupations, as we learn from self-behaviors and others' character and personality. We are all teachers of something.

CHAPTER OVERVIEW

Defining character education and its counterpart character development is provided regarding their onset and culmination. The importance and need for each are emphasized through three examples. Directly following them are the *goals* of the "character" program, which includes self-efficacy and student engagement in learning. These examples include the following: (1) an explanation of sociocentricity, along with the need for persons to follow the golden rule; (2) a teacher's experience regarding the impact of negative (put-down) statements versus positive (lift-up) ones and the purpose and directions for the activity; and (3) information about New York State's teacher candidate mandated program for certification is addressed with an explanation about the importance of thwarting antisocial behaviors in the classroom.

Moral and ethical standards are addressed through the concept of the "hurried child." A culminating thought on why character education and development are necessary in today's society is presented before "A Few Facts about Character Education" is given. These facts have not been provided earlier in the chapter, but are considered very important. This section includes the focus of the chapter, with a few thoughts on how to teach character development and explanation of terms such as being two-faced or sending a mixed message. Comments from colleagues on the social climate of a classroom are provided followed by a quotation from Dr. Martin Luther King before the chapter's closing with "Journal and/or Discussion Questions."

CHARACTER EDUCATION AND CHARACTER DEVELOPMENT: TEACHING AND GROWTH

How does one person or, more specifically, you, educate/teach and develop/grow the qualities of temperament, disposition, or moral fiber? Perhaps the first answer is to know one's own makeup . . . what makes you . . . you. Is it family; the things you own; how you look; your height and/or weight; the clothes you wear; friends; or relationships with others at school, home, or, if you're older, the workplace? Is it all of these things or more? Some see *character education* and its by-product *character development* as an example and outward growth of self-talk, that is, what you think and feel about yourself.

Let's go with that idea, but first reference Dr. Barbara Hayes (2016), a former teacher and school principal, newly retired full-time professor, and presently a field placement supervisor. She commented in a discussion with this author how we often talk about character education and praise its virtues, but questions what we mean by the term. As educators we usually define character education as embodying these traits: kindness, caring, responsibility, good citizenship, fairness, and respect.

However, we agreed that in reality all teachers are teachers of character education. Dr. Hayes stated, "This is done by modeling, setting examples by teachers' everyday actions that they demonstrate to their students their character. It can start out as simply as saying, 'Please' and 'Thank you.' Yet, do children hear these words in their classrooms on a daily basis? You might want to ask your children or ask some adults what they remember about their teachers' character."

WHO'S A TEACHER? WHAT'S CIVILITY?

M. S. Schiering (2000) relates that *everyone is a teacher of something*, and the definition of "character education" lies in training individuals or whole groups to interact with one another in a manner that is friendly and polite, which is *civility*. Subsequently, character education and character development are accomplished by representing and demonstrating good behaviors. Basically, the result of *character education* is *character development* or the exhibition in word and deed of such things, as integrity; being a kind, trustworthy, flexible thinker; and being accepting. With those explanations in mind, the questions next addressed deal with the beginning time and place of *character education*, when it stops, and why there might be a need for it, along with its side effect, *character development*.

THREE QUESTIONS AND ANSWERS ABOUT CHARACTER EDUCATION AND DEVELOPMENT

When Does Character Development Start and Stop?

The "you" of you—a person's character and its subsequent development—is first formed when there is cognition/thinking. It commences in infancy and is a process that takes a lifetime to complete. Subsequently, character education begins when you come into being and doesn't stop until you do. Character development depends on reactions to daily experiences. So, at some juncture, you come to realize that each of us is our experiential past that affects our present and most definitely shapes and impacts our future (see "Daily Experiences" activity at the end of this chapter).

Where Does Character Development Start?

Character development begins in our first surroundings. These could be the place in which you live and it doesn't matter where that is. What does matter is who's around you doing the caregiving and guidance. You become you through the modeling that's presented and how you react to that to form your own personality. An example might be you volunteering your time as you noted adults around you giving their time to help in the community.

Why Might There Be a Need for Character Education/Teaching and Development/Growth?

For those seriously or perhaps even superficially addressing this question, the answer is that there is a need for this type of program, because in order to get along with others, there has to be an example set that provides the components of *civility*. What is that? It's exemplified by behaviors that connote being polite and courteous, having good manners, and showing respect and consideration of oneself and others. Of course, there's selective *civility* where those who know the meaning of the word choose to practice it with some and not with others. Consequently, another need for character teaching and development or growth of character might be learning to converse *with* others as opposed to *at* them or *to* them. Doing so may make it possible to develop caring and respect for oneself, and thereby bring one being a person of good character to those we encounter regularly or now and again, by modeling appropriate behaviors to be emulated.

Overall, addressing this topic of "Why there's a need for character education and development" is a pretty broad matter. If there is a need, then where is that need? This book calls attention to schools' classrooms at the grade one to twelve levels as places for character education. But, those classrooms are a microcosm of a neighborhood, community, city, state, nation, and world. As they stand now, multimedia formats cover and broadcast mostly the horrific things happening around the world. And, on local news stations, the terrible things happening in our immediate communities are given attention. "This hardens us, as we lose our empathy as we are bombarded with negative information. It causes us to be immune to people's hardships" (Meyers 2017a).

So, populations are fed the sensationalism of what's wrong with society. What proliferates is who hates whom and how much. This disdain captures the attention of society as we are ensconced in a comparison of cultures and the right or wrong of one's beliefs and values. Why character education and character development are needed is to thwart the negativity of present-day commonplace social norms. This need is accomplished by providing classrooms that are *safe* and *comfortable* places to be a community of concerned-about-one-another individuals.

The most important thing about any classroom is building community so the student(s) may feel out of harm's way and "protected" in the overall school environment! When these feelings are evidenced, then positive-based social learning and academic instruction are possible.

OVERALL GOAL OF CHARACTER EDUCATION AND DEVELOPMENT: CONSCIOUS WILL

Fundamentally, the goals of character education and development are to provide those experiencing the program with a strong sense of self-worth, self-efficacy, and empowerment. This happens while caring for and about others with whom they attend school, work, or live with at home. Students and/or those being part of this growing-oneself experience become engaged in the learning experience on a social as well as academic level. The place of instruction becomes a comfort zone. Those in it learn about directing their thinking toward the positive with an act of their "conscious will," which is a self-determination act in a way that compliments oneself and others equally. Can this be accomplished? Yes, it is possible to be determined to act in a giving manner and to be part of a comfort zone by creating and owning it. If you question this, "try it and see."

Feelings of those in that setting bring about a sense of security, lack of fear of the unknown, which may be imposed by a more traditional strong emphasis on academics, as opposed to social literacy. The next section explains why there is a need for character education and thereby expands on this section's concepts.

WHY THERE'S A NEED FOR CHARACTER EDUCATION: POINT AND EXAMPLES

Point: Sociocentricity

In a conversation with James Million (2015) this author interpreted his explaining "why" there's a need for character education as being how we, as a society, are moving away from inclusivity to tribalism where there's a kinship to "socio-centricity." The definition of that term involves an individual's need to follow the rules of a group in order to be in the group, as opposed to being excluded from it. At the "being an outsider place" you are then not valued and come to see yourself that way. (Please see chapter 4 for greater detail on sociocentricity and its impact on decision-making.)

Similarly, *tribalism* means our group is the *only* group that has value, truth, or is the one that is right. In tribalism, any invitation to have another point of view is rejected. Subsequently, the need for character education stems from the 'why' as being necessary to avoid divisive behaviors. In Million's opinion, we're in need of such instruction because it proposes the implementation of the golden rule concept: "Do unto others as one wants done unto him or herself." And, let us not forget the need for civility on an ongoing basis.

Example 1: Name-Calling versus "No Put-Downs . . . Only Lift-Ups!": Mid-Career Teaching Story

Mrs. S., previously referred to as "the author," recalls teaching in the late 1970s as one of the first times she realized that there was a huge need for character education and development instruction. The "why" for character education and development was focused on a feeling that had, at its core, a lack of community sense among those she encountered on a daily basis. This was a time when it was commonplace to tell some they were stupid, a messup, or make some derogatory comment. Somehow it was acceptable to make another feel lesser than you in order for you to feel more important. A two-faced mentality was the mainstay, and it wasn't necessarily only school-based but was part of a common social reality everywhere. A sense of community destruction was more the operative than community building.

To counteract this negativity, she incorporated a classroom rule of "No Put-Downs . . . *Only* Lift-Ups!" She placed a banner across the front of the classroom with those words on it. Specifically, the teacher stated that a phrase like "shut up" was not tolerated, as it was a rejection of what someone was saying and definitely a put-down. The idea behind the incorporation of this notion was that, if you couldn't say "shut up," then more severe putdowns might not even be considered. It was a question of focusing on possibly the least damaging of the negative statements being used at that time.

Interestingly, the students knew what put-downs were, but lift-ups needed to be explained as saying phrases like these: "nice job," "I like you," "good work," "be my friend," "I'm proud of you," and "I care about you."

At the beginning of this "one-classroom-statement" implementation, there was tremendous resistance from the students. When Mrs. S. stated that a check mark would be placed next to one's name if she heard anyone say "shut up" or any "put-down," the class challenged her by asking if that was it. "Well," she replied, "I will also *gasp*." Laughter was their response.

The first week there were many who would audibly state a "shut up" put-down. A simple sentence went something like this: "Today, *gasp*, we are going to, *gasp*, list, *gasp*, the subjects, *gasp*, *gasp*, *gasp*, and predicates from these ten sentences in, *gasp*, two columns on, *gasp*, the board." Laryngitis and her overall speech pattern were severely compromised that week, to say the least.

The students got tired of the teacher's gasping and her placing "check marks" next to a person's name for saying a put-down. Their testing her this way got to be boring. Although it was sort of a game to see if she'd put down a check mark the fun wasn't that much fun. Interestingly, the second week found the students tattling on one another with statements like, "She said 'it!'" The reply was: "It's okay to say the word 'it,' but what are words we are not to say?" The students answered, "No way we're saying those two words!" Tattling proliferated that second week, but at least the gasping was done.

Ah, the third week was the height of cleverness. The students could not be heard saying "shut up." No, they could be seen mouthing the words. No sound, no gasp, no check mark. And by week four, no one bothered to do anything. The 120 students seen throughout the day simply didn't say "shut up" and in time didn't use other put-downs, at least not when with this educator.

Fascinatingly, a student came forward some weeks after the aforementioned rule was applied and said that he'd been told to "shut up" by the person he'd sat next to in the cafeteria for lunch each day. Well, that and a few other expletives were spoken. The teacher asked how he reacted, and the boy, Tim, explained that he told the kid he couldn't say "shut up" because Mrs. S. doesn't allow it. "Well, I'm not in her class, so I can say whatever I want!" was the reply. "Yeah, but I am in her class and I don't have to listen to it," he said as he moved to another table. It appeared that the idea of no put-downs was spreading to others.

Larry, a student in third period English Language Arts, practiced no put-downs, and took the rule home with him. The teacher found this out when she received a phone call at her home from his dad. It went like this:

"Hello, is this Mrs. S.?"

"Yes, and this is?"

"I'm Larry's dad. You know, Larry from your class. He told me that I can't tell him to shut up, that it's not right."

Gasping, Mrs. S. replied, "You did that? Why? Larry loves you and wants you to hear what he has to say. He cares about you, and you are so important to him. What would you do if he said those words to you?"

"I'd smack him across the face" was the quick answer.

"I'm sorry, clearly our classroom statement/rule bothers you and, really, I was just trying to have the students be civil to one another to build classroom community and know that we care about one another enough to listen and not put anyone down."

Larry's dad was silent, and then he said, "I bet you think you're clever!" Larry's dad then abruptly slammed down the phone to end the call.

Mrs. S. thought to call back, but refrained from doing so while ruminating over the call and what might have been said. She worried all night. When she saw Larry in class the next day she apologized for causing him any trouble at home the previous night. And, Larry responded with how his dad walked out of the room while he stayed watching television. An hour later, he related that his dad came over to the television, stood in front of it so Larry couldn't see the screen, turned off the sound, and said, "I'm sorry, son, I should not have said that, and I won't do that again. Now, let me hear what you were going to tell me earlier tonight."

Mrs. S., when hearing what happened, thought how bad things might have turned out and was totally relieved that, in this case, the message of positivity had come across, and Larry and his dad had had a good conversation. By mid-year, many teachers had the "No Put-Downs . . . *Only* Lift-Ups" banner in their classrooms. The one statement turned into a life lesson about a way to live civilly, that makes one feel good about self and others, when practiced.

Mrs. S. still teaches and practices this form of character development, explaining that it's not just for someone else but for one's self as well.

The self-talk should be: "Don't put yourself down, as it serves no purpose" (M. S. Schiering 1976).

"This classroom '. . . Only lift ups' rule is the core of building a classroom community and civility existing there. Character education and development, with this rule in place, provides a location where one can feel accepted as he/she is, regardless of ability level, culture, ethnicity, or the other things that seem to separate one from another. Basically, everyone wants acceptance, everyone is a teacher of something, and everyone is a learner as well. How you act sets an example for others and if you're lifting someone's spirits as well as your own, the result is you feel good" (M. S. Schiering 1999–present).

CLASSROOM, HOME, OR CHARACTER EDUCATION WORKSHOP ACTIVITY: PUT-DOWNS AND LIFT-UPS!

Figure 1.1.   "Scars on the Heart" (M. S. Schiering 2000)

Activity Purpose

This first activity in this book serves as a beginning for character education and development training. The Scars on the Heart (figure 1.1) activity was provided to bring awareness to how words hurt and how the hurt remains for a long time, depending on who delivered the hurting statement. When one feels diminished by negativity coming from parents, peers, or a person who matters, the impact of the hurt shapes behaviors that may well bring hurtful statements to another when sharing occurs.

Activity Directions

If you're in a classroom or conducting a workshop and want to emphasize the effect of the afore-mentioned quotation, follow these steps:

1. Make a large paper heart.
2. Have all in the group write or print their first name somewhere on the heart. Be sure to put your name on it as well.
3. Instruct the group to make "put-down" statements, and explain that you will not take these personally. Of course, cursing is definitely not permitted.
4. Each time a negative statement is made, fold the paper heart, one little fold at a time, until the paper heart is tiny and not discernible as having a heart shape.
5. Now, ask for positive statements or "lift-ups." Explain that you will take each one personally. When each statement is given, be sure to *unfold* a part of the heart that you previously folded.
6. Show the unfolded heart to the group, and ask what is seen. Wait for responses, which should be that there are lines all over the heart.
7. Explain that these lines are called "scars on the heart." Further emphasize that it matters not how many times there was a positive statement, you could have a hundred of these, but the scars cannot be removed or eradicated. They just remain there, impacting you negatively.
8. Mention that you once heard that if a negative statement is delivered by someone who doesn't matter to you, the effect will last for three to five years. However, if the negative statement was delivered by someone for whom you care, then the scar lasts from ten years to a lifetime.
9. Mention that negativity hurts feelings and influences one's thinking, usually not for the betterment of one's self-image.

Example 2: New York State Education Department's Dignity for All Students Act (DASA)

In December of 2013, New York State Education Department incorporated a teacher candidate mandatory workshop addressing "Dignity for All

Students." Additionally, all schools in grades one through twelve were to
have representatives to whom students could report to if their "dignity"
had been compromised through the practice of harassment, bullying, cyber-
bullying, prejudice, and/or discrimination (see "Definition of Antisocial
Behaviors" in the next section). This author, for her college, wrote a syllabus
and has served as the instructor for the seven-hour DASA workshop since it
started and through the present time.

Why did the state incorporate the character education training in all
schools: public, charter, or private? Why did the state bring attention to the
necessity for ensuring that being a person of good character is a necessary
practice? The answer is that antisocial behaviors are considered absolutely
not acceptable! Subsequently, the state deemed that behavior training/charac-
ter development, along with supportive intervention or mediation, is required
for maintaining a positive learning environment for all students. This character development is incorporated where conflict has or hasn't arisen, with
behavior management as the resultant vehicle for correction of inappropriate
ways of conducting oneself.

Interestingly, while the prevention of these character traits is being
addressed in schools in the aforementioned grades, it is also being addressed
through *Title Nine* at the college/university level for those working in these
environments.

DASA established codes of conduct that prohibited the aforementioned
antisocial behaviors by students and/or school employees on school property,
or at a school function while being there or transported to it. Definitions from
DASA were provided for clarification of its terms regarding what was meant
by school property and functions, types of disability, forms of discrimination,
physical and emotional harm, as well as gender. A positive learning environment, the state proclaimed, must be provided and maintained at all times. If
an entire state incorporates into every grade-level's curriculum a workshop
addressing character education for development of one's character, then these
two are envisioned as being "needed" in our schools.

DEFINITION OF ANTISOCIAL BEHAVIORS: (NEW YORK STATE EDUCATION DEPARTMENT 2013)

The Dignity for All Students Act of the New York State Education Department has definitions of anti-social behaviors. This author (2013) consolidated
these for the state-mandated DASA Workshop as follows:

Harassment. This is the creation of a hostile environment by conduct or by
threats, intimidation or abuse, including those behaviors that interfere with
a student's educational performance; opportunities or benefits; or mental,

emotional, or physical well-being, or cause one to fear for his or her physical safety, or emotional harm, which may occur "off school property." But this emotional harm would create a risk of substantial disruption *within* the school environment. It is that school environment where that conduct, treatment of another through pestering, being a nuisance, annoying, stalking, or persecution occurs.

Nonverbal harassment might also be considered to cause the aforementioned emotional harm making the school environment to be uncomfortable, because of someone continually being indifferent to someone or ignoring that person or persons. This author refers to nonverbal harassment as giving someone the "silent treatment" and/or demonstrating indifference or ignoring him or her.

Bullying. This is maltreatment or singling out a person and hounding that person. The idea is that the person being bullied is different from the one delivering the bullying, because of attitude perceived or actual religion, color, ethnic group, disability, sexual orientation, gender (identity and expression), and/or one's age, level of education, or test scores (high or low), to name a few considerations. Overall, bullying is a form of harassment and discrimination.

Cyber-Bullying. This is a means of bullying using the Internet and social media networks. (See chapter 3 for more information regarding this topic.)

Discrimination. This is the act of favoritism, bias, bigotry, and/or intolerance.

Prejudice. This is the discrimination or thoughts regarding bias, intolerance, unfairness, and/or bigotry displayed toward another person, which is based on one's beliefs about that individual's being different to oneself, because of the items mentioned in bullying.

Think about It: Character education and the accompanying character development are vitally necessary in today's schools, because in the past fifteen to twenty years the beliefs and values taught at home are not essentially what were previously experienced. Whatever the cause, there have been reports regarding moral and ethical standards waning on an international plane. Just over a decade ago, *USA Today* magazine reported on school-related bullying resulting in violence with twenty-seven children killed by schoolmates, and an equal number injured, in the past ten years. Fourteen years ago, Britzman and Hanson (2003) summed up the current state of affairs: "While our present society places enormous academic pressure on children, this is often at the expense of character development."

And David Elkind (1981/2001) related in his original 1981 book *The Hurried Child: Growing Up Too Fast Too Soon* the need for character education when he referenced that children aren't learning the means of social discourse. He stated, "The real danger of growing up fast is that children learn the rules of social license before they learn the rules of mutual respect" (M. S. Schiering 2009, 68).

Dr. Joanne O'Brien (2016), associate dean in the Division of Education at Molloy College, sums up the need for instruction about being a person of good character when she states, "Character development is needed in our schools to help develop the qualities, in all of our students, and us as well, which most people uphold as being integral to being a member of a *civil* and *humane* society."

A Few Facts about Character Education

The main focus of this chapter was to relate the need for character education and its accompanying character development. This task was done with regard to the need for learning about what it is to be a person of good character relying on several factors. Not presented previously, these factors include those presented at character development workshops through Project SAVE and at other places over the years, as well as in 2016, as presentations on character development (M. S. Schiering 2000, 2016a, 2016b, 2016c):

1. A basic awareness is required that character development comprehension may be recognized as a process that might encompass the early childhood, preadolescent, adolescent, and adult years, taking a lifetime to complete.
2. Character development is a learned response that becomes more natural as it's practiced.
3. Having life experiences upon which one can reflect, synthesize, and analyze the information helps to develop one's being a person of good character.
4. There are certain crucial life experiences that all cultures embrace. These are birth, death, success, failure, tradition, and love (Dewey 1937). (These life experiences are further discussed in chapter 5.)

COGNITION PROBLEM: BEING TWO FACED

A social cognition problem that seemingly exists everywhere, regardless of age or grade levels, is that of being *two-faced*. Recently a friend told me of work she'd done for her job and how there was praise or acknowledgment given by the director. She later came to discover that others to whom she reported about her work had taken credit for her work and had made put-down statements about her in the process. Her lack of trusting followed and continued from this incident for over ten years.

Along the same lines, a mom told me about how her son was told by a classmate how he'd done so well on the test and that was so "cool." However, when he wasn't seen on the playground but witnessed this individual and another classmate talking, he heard the one who remarked about his being "cool" say the exact opposite with a statement that went like this: "Did you see that test score 'T' got; he is really stupid because you know how he got the high score? He totally cheated off my paper. He's so stupid."

Social Cognition Problem: Mixed Messages

Sometimes a person confuses how another feels by giving two contradictory statements to the same person. For this section the focus is on a mixed message for an individual. This practice can actually be done through words or actions, or both. A very simple example is telling someone you are concerned with his or her well-being and then ignoring that person, being indifferent when he or she says that he or she doesn't feel well, and not asking how he or she is doing, or just walking away. Sometimes a mixed message is saying one thing and having a facial expression that doesn't match what is being said. For example, a teacher might say to a student that his or her work is good but shows a frown, as opposed to a smile on his or her face. Which message is correct? Are the spoken words or the facial expression indicative of what's being meant?

WHAT A SCHOOL SHOULD BE: AUTHOR'S OPINION

Schools are what can be and should be, in this author's opinion, the neutral meeting ground for varied cultures, dispositions, and belief and value systems. "Yet schools are frequently recognized as being far less than a neutral meeting ground because of the numerous reports on lack of ethics and moral substance within the public and private sectors" (O'Connor-Petruso et al. 2004, 4). Why is there such segregation instead of neutrality or a desire to have a mutual respect for those different from oneself, or those belonging to a different group?

One answer may be that news programs, in whatever format, do not emphasize the good of human nature, but rather the negativity. A moral code of conduct, one taught in the home and supported in schools, is seemingly marginalized by the emphasis on negativity and/or emphasis on students' academic standings, as opposed to social discourse ones. The idea of test scores that are taking precedence over caring about those around us would require a refocusing on what's truly important and that's an affable classroom community that enhances learning. With this thought in mind, Dr. Madeline

Craig (2016) explains that probably, the enrichment of learning would result, in elevated test scores so the two, scores and sense of well-being/community, could coexist harmoniously in the classroom.

Ask adults over the age of forty what was the most important thing about schools, and they'll recall the socialization and not the test scores. Yet, in today's society, the valuing of test scores, it seems, has taken precedence over getting along with others. In the long run, the students who learn are those who are comfortable in the classroom, and those are the students where a teacher has taken the time to build a caring community.

As Connolly and Giouroukakis (2016) state in their book about the proliferation of test-taking "good education would require coming up with many different answers representing a range of values and viewpoints. And, "come to understand other perspectives and cultures through evaluation of their own perspectives and the perspectives of others." This author recognizes that these ideas deal with test taking and social literacy regarding what a school should be—not emphasizing test scores, but allowing for in-class communication/social literacy as well to have an equal place in the classroom.

QUOTATION: DR. MARTIN LUTHER KING JR.

As Dr. Martin Luther King Jr. wrote as far back as 1947 regarding the purpose of education, "We must remember that intelligence is not enough. Intelligence plus character—that is the goal of true education." To King's quotation this author adds, "We have control over our behavior with modeling positive character traits. This is accomplished through acts of our conscious will" (2000-present). Looking at the two quotations from 2016 and 1947, nearly seventy years apart, it stands to reason that the teachings of the former impacted this author's thinking about the importance of the true goal of education.

JOURNAL AND/OR DISCUSSION QUESTIONS

1. What is meant by character education and character development, and why do you think there's a need for them in schools?
2. What do you suppose is meant by the idea of "everyone is a teacher of something"?
3. What's your reaction to the "No put-downs . . . *Only* lift-ups!" concept?
4. What does it mean to be two-faced, and what is meant by mixed messages?
5. In your opinion, what does it mean to have a civil society, and how do you suppose Dr. King's statement might influence that idea?

Chapter 2

Getting to Know You

CHAPTER OVERVIEW

The chapter commences with an invitation to address the importance of one's own character as an educator and/or learner. Definitions or explanations that assist in clarifying learning and teaching are provided, as one's cultural influences are addressed. Then, the question of how you, the reader, teacher, or learner, feel about yourself is asked. Examples of experiences that resulted in shaping thoughts and feelings and helped establish two individuals' personal viewpoints are provided on: (1) letting go, (2) one's feeling secure, and then (3) balancing one's daily routine.

The difference between talking with others and being a passive recipient of information is provided. Conversing "with" someone, as opposed to "at" or "to" individuals is given attention. Conversation comes before an activity dealing with "getting acquainted." This activity's purpose and directions for implementation are provided. The chapter closes with "Journal and/or Discussion Questions."

YOUR OWN CHARACTER

You're now invited to address the importance of your own character as an educator, learner and/or one teaching character development in a classroom or workshop. The school is the place where teaching and learning are most commonly recognized as taking place. However, wherever we are or whomever we are with, aside from our own behaviors, there are the actions and words of others that serve to teach each of us about us. This is experienced through our reactions to what these persons say and do and their priority in our lives. These spoken or implied thoughts and feelings help to provide us with and/or establish our own sense of self.

So, how do you see yourself? Is your mind swimming with a multitude of thoughts in order to answer that question? In all likelihood, it is, and that's because we are complex individuals who seem to become more multifaceted as time elapses. The intricacy of self is a result of experiences we have that shape us as individuals and the talking we do with ourselves (self-talk). And, it's the intertwining of what we think and feel regarding those experiences that compounds that impression of "who" we are.

Knowing who one is, and from where those perceptions developed, profoundly influences an individual's attitudes and how one teaches and/or sets a behavioral example for those being taught. Subsequently, it's important to know yourself to know about the "how" of teaching about character and its growth.

A LITTLE BIT ABOUT LEARNING

Learning involves making the connections between thinking and comprehension so that one develops cognition skills that are able to be transferred to everyday situations. "Learning is connected to reflective intelligence and affected by self-awareness, beliefs about one's abilities, clarity and strength of learning goals, personal expectations, and motivation to know about things" (Abbott 1994). Learning, overall, is a social experience that occurs oftentimes in a social setting, such as a classroom.

With the aforementioned involvements in a social setting, there ensues in that setting an interaction between and among learners as meanings are shared. "Learning is a natural process; it is not an activity such as something a person does when they don't do something else. It isn't something that one customarily stops and does, but rather a process of learning that happens everywhere and at different levels, individually, collectively and most profoundly, socially" (Wenger 1998, 227; 2006).

"Learning may be defined as a modification in disposition or capability, which can be retained" (Gagné 1977). During this changing process, a person may learn, but his or her conduct may not be altered while his or her attitude does show this. The appeal of defining learning as a change in behavior, performance, actions, manner, or an observable change in one's disposition is obvious. Recognizing learning as observable change allows it to be measured and, therefore verified. "At its foundation learning is a complex phenomenon that is influenced by many factors, such as its being a reconstruction of past experience that influences individuals' and whole groups' behavior and dispositions" (M. S. Schiering, Bogner, and Buli-Holmberg 2011).

A LITTLE BIT ABOUT TEACHING

Teaching is the act of passing on information for learning. Of course, that's a rather simplistic explanation, as the process of passing along information may be done in a multitude of ways. "Most importantly, teaching is defined or explained by the style of delivery and attention to learners' needs that one uses on a regular basis in the classroom or other setting where learning occurs" (M. S. Schiering 2003). Haugsbakk and Nordkvelle (2007), as referenced in the aforementioned citation, relate that teaching is the facilitation or assisting processes one employs for learning.

CULTURAL INFLUENCES OF LEARNING, TEACHING, AND YOUR CHARACTER

Thinking about culture with respect to teaching and learning, one may consider it as a medium for growing things (Eisner 1997, 353). For each person in the school setting, there is a mutual exchange with an intertwining of the "roles" each is expected to play. "In a fashion, we are growing students as we ourselves grow, so that who we are as learners and teachers is in a state of culturally-influenced learning, and teaching interaction" (M. S. Schiering 2002, 554).

Eisner (1997, 349–53) explains culture when he states, "In the anthropological sense, a culture is a shared way of life, and encompasses the art, beliefs, behaviors and idea of a particular society." Generally, the difference in students who are culturally based is reliant on what's called the "Phenomenological Perspective—the study of perceptual experience in a purely subjective format" (Trigwell and Prosser 1997, 241–52; M. S. Schiering 1999, 28; 2003, 555, 556, 558). This perspective is a descriptive or classificatory account of any life event that is apparent to the senses. Subjectivism, it is realized, provides a natural reaction to situations, often grounded in cultural mores.

Cultural influences may include such things as: style of clothing one wears, preferred foods, activities such as sports, ways of communicating that involve eye contact and body stance, sentence structure and language expressions, as much as forms of entertainment, recognized and celebrated traditions, and qualifications for what it means to succeed.

Not only are cultural mores part of one's experience but also the differences of these in a classroom are to be recognized as influencing conversations that demonstrate one's character. Other discourse impacts include books one reads, television programs that one views, reports on current events, situational comedies, drama, or the like. Also, there is internet research, video games, and the myriad of overt and subliminal communication that's experienced on a daily basis through social media text messaging, and so forth.

Each should be taken into account when addressing "who" one is as a learner and teacher, the "you" of you.

Social and societal contexts form and have formed, shape and have shaped the physical, cognitive, and emotional learning environment we have come to create as parents, siblings, relatives, friends, teachers, community members, or even strangers (M. S. Schiering 2003, 554).

NOW THOUGHTS: WHAT DO YOU THINK AND FEEL ABOUT YOURSELF?

What you think and feel about yourself impacts character education and most importantly character development in everyday situations. This impact is because you set an example to which others will respond. The reaction may be positive or negative, or somewhere in between those places. Nonetheless, a reaction will occur. If you're a teacher in a grade one to twelve classroom or college, the way you represent yourself will influence others as assuredly as the sun rises. How you present yourself becomes the "you" of you, as others remember how you made them feel. As Angelou (2007) stated in *The Village Voice*, "People may forget what you did. People may forget what you said. But people will never forget how you made them feel."

If you think back to teachers you had in previous years or even this one, if you're still in school, you may not recall the name of the educator, but you will recall the comfort level in that classroom. So, while you're setting an example, you are formed by the ones you experienced. Remember, we're all teachers of something.

Some food for thought is to note whether you exhibit character traits that include your being caring, giving, concerned, trustworthy, responsible, kind, tolerant, and polite. Those are just a few that people connote with being a good person. If you do have these traits, then you're on the right track for teaching character education. If, however, you are one who contrasts students or yourself to others, in a negative manner, or if you pit one person against another, or talk negatively behind someone's back, then be aware that your behavior is observable and noted. Teaching character development means modeling being a person of good character.

Primarily, any of this section's questions may be answered with the current "you" based on what you remember, those experiences that were important enough for you to recall. This author has, over the past twenty years, written and conducted workshops stating, "What you think and feel becomes what you say and do!" Now, you're asked to examine the things you think and feel and how they came to be. In all likelihood, these happened through realizing what's important to you based on your accumulated daily experiences, the reason "why" you are who you are. To provide an example, you're asked to think back to your learning how to ride a bicycle.

ONE WOMAN'S LEARNING EXPERIENCE: FIRST BICYCLE RIDE—REFLECTION REALIZATION

For the over 3,000 students I've taught, including the persons in workshops on character education, this singular "first bicycle ride" experience can be recalled without hesitation. One woman, around age fifty or sixty, explained to a group that she remembered her dad holding onto the back of the bicycle seat as she peddled and he ran next to her: "I was around age seven when this happened. When I realized he'd let go of the seat, suddenly, the handlebars I was gripping, wobbled. It was then that I fell off the bike."

Her dad, running to her side, asked what had happened. She replied, "You let go!"

Her dad answered, "Yes, you were doing so well I thought you'd be fine."

Crying at the time of this experience, the woman further explained that she then told her dad that she'd expected him to hold onto the bicycle seat until she felt *secure*. "And, when do you suppose that secure feeling would happen?," he asked.

She replied through a seven-year-old's tear-stained eyes: "I thought that'd be somewhere around age twelve."

Those hearing the story broke into laughter, but the impact of that time had stayed with the woman for over forty years. Why? The impact of that time was so important that she could recall that incident in detail. What she came to share further was that she realized that she needed her dad to be there for her, not just to assist her in riding that bicycle, but in most things, until she was ready to let go. "Ah, letting go," she came to relate, was of huge significance with her. Being able to do that is something she has had to deal with for a long time.

As teachers, do we know this about our students, with what issues they deal on a regular basis? Are they able to *let go of negativity* or things that happened that weren't so positive? If not, why not? And, do we know what makes them feel secure in the classroom? Why or why not? "People are complex. Every one of us has rich backgrounds full of emotional wealth. These emotional experiences shape us . . . how we feel about ourselves, and how we relate to others as well" (Meyers 2017b).

It is such experiences as the one exemplified in the anecdote that make the "you" of you. As you reflect on these past experiences, silently, for a moment, what are some experiences that come to your mind that helped shape your personality? And, now, just for a further experiment, you are asked to think of something this past week or so that was of significance to you. What is something you learned from that experience that you think might stay with you for some time to come?

A LEARNING EXPERIENCE EXAMPLE: REFLECTION REALIZATION, LAUREN S.—AGE TWENTY-TWO

When asked the question about something she'd learned in the past week or so, during the school winter break from student teaching, Lauren Spotkov (2016) replied with "I learned about the importance of balance. I don't mean the type you do when trying to stand on a balance beam or balancing yourself so you don't fall off something. I am referring to the type that involves time distribution.

"Over this vacation period I stayed at home and had a lot of time to think. This past semester with college requirements I was spending my time studying, writing lesson plans, doing demonstration lessons and then holding down a part time job. So, thinking and being with just me wasn't part of my experience. What I realized was how much time I spent being responsible and doing what was expected of me to maintain my status at school and have an income, of sorts. What I learned was that I have nearly always spent my time at college . . . at least more than anywhere else.

"Even though I think that education is of the highest value, as I reflected over vacation, I now realize there are many other important aspects of my life. These include spending time with others, talking with people, forming relationships, and maintaining or recapturing former ones. Balance of one's time is very important, and I learned a life lesson that involves where I place my priorities."

DIFFERENCES BETWEEN CONVERSING AND BEING PASSIVE RECIPIENTS OF INFORMATION

At the onset, before the following activity takes place, be sure to realize and instruct those involved that there is a difference between talking "to" and "at" someone and conversing "with" others. The last of these is vital, as the first two are simply means for dissemination of topic(s) for the taking-in of material. In fact, one is merely being a "passive recipient" when talked to or at. If you are in a classroom, you may recognize these as times when instructions are being provided for a project or assignment. And, if at home, maybe instructions are given on how to do a chore, prepare a meal, and help out when needed. Talking "to" or "at" others is very commonplace!

Talking with others, that is, holding a back and forth give-and-take, conversationally, is uncommon. Why, because we have become accustomed to particular patterns and rarely go beyond them. Subsequently, we do not get to know others, but rather only see the product produced by their endeavors or for that matter, lack of producing something.

CLASSROOM, HOME, OR CHARACTER EDUCATION WORKSHOP ACTIVITY: GETTING ACQUAINTED

Figure 2.1.   Getting Acquainted:—Sticky Hands Two

Activity Purpose

This activity's purpose is to have those doing it getting to know one another in a social context. It focuses on sharing some cultural influences and/or favorite sports, in- or after-school activities, vacations, family members, and generic life experiences that have shaped the "you" of you. This is the title of chapter 2 with getting to know one another and discovering who the people in your neighborhood are, meaning the people you're with presently.

Activity Directions

This is a kinesthetic activity in that participants first get up out of their seats to then march around the room. With someone selected as line leader, the class marches behind this individual until the teacher calls out "Sticky Hands Two." It is at this point that each member of the assemblage finds a partner and faces this person with their fingertips touching one another as seen in figure 2.1.

This is the time for an exchange of information beginning with stating your name. Then, topics such as family members and birth order are exchanged. This information is followed by such things as favorite sports, pets, vacation spots, books read, and subject area most preferred, as conversations begin and are extended until the leader of the activity says, "Sticky Hands Three." Then, each group member is to find two new people with whom they'll provide the same information. Getting acquainted is the operative. Hand washing is recommended directly before and after this activity.

JOURNAL AND/OR DISCUSSION QUESTIONS

1. What are some thoughts and feelings you had about yourself after reading this chapter?
2. How might the "you" of you influence you teaching character development?
3. What was your reaction to the "Bicycle" story and why do you suppose you reacted that way?
4. How would you define "having a conversation?"
5. In the "Getting Acquainted" activity, what did you learn from the sharing and how do you suppose this might impact your personality?
6. What were some thoughts or opinions you had about Lauren's learning to balance her time?

Chapter 3

What Are You Thinking?

CHAPTER OVERVIEW

The chapter commences with the authors viewpoint on the *atmosphere* of a classroom being vital as to whether or not learning is happening or will occur in that setting. An example simile is provided. Then, it's explained that being a person of good character is seen to be at the heart of what matters. Next, a social cognition model is addressed in an illustrative format.

The definition of a learning model is provided with an example of how it's owned. Then the history of this particular model is addressed before a narrative about the model's foundation of "reflection" is explained as impacting on thinking and feelings, which form the cognitive collective. Types of thinking and feelings are given attention as each plays a role in social realities, in such places as the school's classrooms. The difference between thinking/cognition skills and feelings is addressed. Basically, the construction of one's temperament relies on the differentiation of thoughts, ideas, opinions, judgments, and feelings (Schiering and Bogner 2011).

Two activities requiring group interaction follow the identification of thinking terms. The purpose and directions of the activities are provided. The first interaction involves being in a classroom where social cognition is as much a mainstay as academics. This small-group, and later whole-class, activity, calls for the recognition of social thinking. The next interaction involves recalling daily experiences that helped shape one's beliefs and/or values, and/or behavior traits. The chapter concludes with "Journal and/or Discussion Questions."

CLASSROOM ATMOSPHERE

This author believes that in a society that is seemingly predicated on negativity, character education and *ethical codes of conduct* encapsulate our lives. These are realized most emphatically in classrooms across our country. This morality issue is recognized regardless of where a person resides. Character instruction and growth are at the heart of what matters in school. This type of instruction underpins math, science, social studies, reading, or language arts, the main curriculum topics. "Why?" You may wonder. The answer is because in order to learn, the student must first feel not just physically comfortable, but most importantly emotionally comfortable, contented, and secure in the classroom. Any type of discomfort serves as an impediment to learning.

Example: Simile

Think of what you're like when you are thirsty or maybe even hungry and you're in a classroom, or for that matter, anywhere you're involved in an activity in or outside the home. What are you thinking? Does it matter what subject matter is being taught, or what's going on around you? Where is your focus? In all likelihood you are concentrating on getting your thirst quenched and/or your appetite satisfied. Until those biological needs are met, the subject matter being taught or the activity in which you're involved, takes second place.

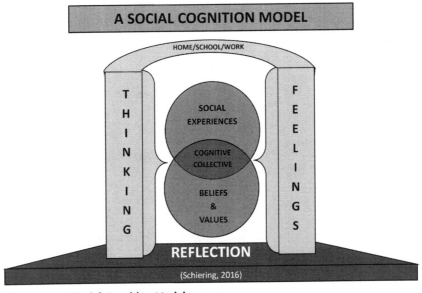

Figure 3.1. A Social Cognition Model

Specifically, how you feel in a classroom, if learning is to occur, must embrace feelings of comfort, relaxation, and security. These are biological emotional needs involving mental sustenance, which are as important as the basic human needs of food, clothing and shelter. If surrounded and absorbed in comfort, due to the persons in the classroom having and acting on positive character traits, then learning occurs! And, if not, then the converse is usually the case.

THE REASON FOR THE MODEL

Before getting heavily into defining a model and the components of this model, the author expresses here the reason for the model. It came into thought and then configuration, due in large part to the advancement of computer technology in society and especially the classroom. While the Internet became more accessible and handheld devices proliferated in our cultures, there came to be less communication. Certainly, there was less communication with others being evidenced. Civil was omitted from civilization as courses in civics were no longer part of most school curricula. Information gathering and distribution were done, for the most part, online, as opposed to having conversations with others.

Definition of a Learning Model with an Example

"The noun, model, implies an active and personal construction of one's own theory, as well as its inevitable change in content and function with experience" (Bretherton 1985, 33). That's a relatively simple way of explaining a model of learning and its reciprocal function of teaching, addressing, in this case, the social aspect of a classroom. In order for a model to be effective, it must be accessible to learners with a sense-of-ownership happening.

A summary of defining this "ownership" concept was provided by Borkowski et al. (1989, 64). Paraphrased, these authors relate that it's recognized that one has, when using a model, a pervading attitude that this model belongs to the user, because of adhering to its concepts and personalizing it: "To own a model, in this sense, implies that a teacher/student must practice its major components, receive guidance in modifying related instructional techniques, adapt the model's characteristics to the unique circumstances of the classroom, and update the model based on personal experiences" (Borkowski 1992/2011, 253).

You might look at a learning model for social cognition as being similar to constructing something using Lego blocks. First, you go to the store and select the exact model you want. Since there's a picture on the box's cover, you find this selection rather easy. Then, with your model preference in hand, you open the box at home. Here you begin to put it together, realizing that someone put all the pieces you need to construct this item in the package for you, along with some instructions that are not in words but visually explained, step by step. Working diligently, you put each piece together until you have the completed model, ready to look at and use. It's yours, and you made it. You take ownership of it!

Next, a friend comes over, and you play with the model together. You take turns and enjoy the experience. Each of you takes ownership of the model in using it during the time you're sharing. A learning model is like that, as when you use it, it belongs to you. Maybe you'll make your own model one day and maybe not. Nonetheless, it's yours while you use it.

Model's Beginning/History

The idea for this social cognition learning model began in the 1990s and then blossomed into presentations and magazine articles about it in varied locations and publications in the United States, South America, Great Britain, and parts of Norway; starting in 2002. It was copyrighted in 2003 by this author, as a portion of a model addressing academic as well as social cognition. In 2008, with colleagues Dr. Drew Bogner and instructor Jorun Buli-Holmberg, two modifications were made to the academic and social cognition model, and that revised model was published in 2011 by Rowman and Littlefield as *Teaching and Learning: A Model for Academic and Social Cognition*.

The core of this model was then extrapolated and put back into its original form with graphic design assistance from Rickey Moroney (2017) and attention given to the social atmosphere of a classroom. This atmosphere underpinned any academic topics with respect to, as stated in chapters one and two, the need for a student learner to feel comfortable in a learning setting in order to learn effectively.

EXPLAINING THE MODEL

Reflection: Social Cognition Learning Model's Foundation

If one looks up the synonyms for the word *reflection*, there's mention of these: likeness, indication, sign, manifestation, suggestion, expression, evidence, signal, consideration, thinking, thought, contemplation, deliberation, musing, and rumination. Examining those, this author adds an explanation of reflection as being individuals and whole societies' thinking about former and future events in their lives. In a manner of speaking, each of us is a by-product of our individual and shared past experiences.

Why, you may question, and the answer would be that *who* one is now is reliant on memories and the emotional, as well as cognitive, reactions to past situations. These could involve family, school, community, national, and world events, as easily as friendships, relationships of significance, places visited, and just about anything. When one recalls any of the aforementioned and thinks about them and realizes the feelings associated with them for an extended period of time, one has reflection or the act of reflecting.

As stated earlier in this book, "We are our experiential past." (M. S. Schiering, 2000). In *Teaching and Learning: A Model for Academic and Social Cognition* M.S. Schiering (2003, 558–59) comments, "People can only address, perceive particulars, configure generalities, respond through emotions and interpret what they find to be important in their life experience through the viewing—reflection on previous experiences. One's points-of-reference are based upon his reflection."

Looking back at our experiences impacts our present personality, our character, as these happenings have made us *who* we are and impact on the decisions we make for the future, or even, present time. Reflection on our life experiences and/or "students, with respect to what they bring into classrooms; their feelings, thoughts attitudes and belief and value systems, and the way in which these impact learning, influences and shapes that environment."

Bogner (2008/2011) states, "As teachers, we are engaged in a noble undertaking, wrestling with the vastly varying dreams, hopes, and beliefs of individuals and society, helping to fashion anew each day a different but connected reality for improving the task of learning and teaching." The learning model in figure 3.1 has the overall term of "reflection," because it is this mental process that substantially forms the "you" of each of us.

The Cognitive Collective: Model's Interior Component

In a poem by this author in the late to mid-1990s, the last line reads, "We are a combination of what we think and feel." With that in mind, the cognitive collective is explained as the connection of thoughts, ideas, opinions, judgments, and feelings, or the "interaction/interplay" between them. In the social cognition model of this book, the thinking and feelings done about beliefs and values, as well as social experiences, overlap to form the core of this social learning model.

An individual's meaning is constructed with reflective reactions to the components of the cognitive collective, which are continually addressed, consciously with awareness or unawareness; thinking is nearly always happening. The importance of social cognition to institute social change relies on these reciprocal and symbiotic processes. They need to be held onto and serve as the guardian of individuals' modified or newly evidenced experiential responses to situations being of a positive nature—*your positive nature.*

Prior to delving into the examples and impact of these two overlapping components, Schiering and Bogner (2011/2015, in *Teaching and Learning: A Model for Academic and Social Cognition* and Learning and Teaching Creative Cognition: The Interactive Book Report) define the cognitive collective's thinking and feelings as follows:

1. *Thoughts:* Immediate conscious responses to reflection, which involve memory. Reflection is further defined by Schon (1997) as having two forms, which are reflection "in" action, or thoughts occurring now in the present, and reflection "on" action, as referencing something that happened in the past.
2. *Ideas:* A prediction of future responses or speculation based on one's perspective as a result of reflection.
3. *Opinions:* A combination of thoughts and ideas in that a formulated concept results.
4. *Judgments:* Concretized or solidified thoughts, ideas, and opinions that are impacted by memory, while being based on reflection concerning past experiences. Often, these are based upon one's level of attachment to a situation. Judgments are not easily changed, but they may well change. If judgments are easily modified, then you've expressed a thought, idea, or opinion, as opposed to a judgment.

(See appendix A for a graphic organizer addressing reciprocal thinking and a more definitive explanation of this portion of the social cognition model. Then, definitions for each thinking skill, whether in the beginning awareness, creative and critical thinking, or the meta-cognitive processes phases are provided.)

5. *Feelings:* A sensory and/or emotional response to stimuli that may be descriptive or classificatory. Feelings are also defined as being the quality that something has in that one responds in a manner that connotes feeling of an emotional or intuitive nature and/or reflects on something to establish a formed response that is grounded in one's thoughts, ideas, opinions, and judgments.

"Subsequently, feelings and emotions are one and the same and can be observed or defined as being joined. These then are trans-rational responses to stimuli in that a sensory response to situations occurs at the same juncture as deeply held thoughts, ideas, opinions, and judgments. Feelings/emotions may be seen as 'root responses' to stimuli" (Bogner 2011a).

"Feelings just exist, and are envisioned as neither being right nor wrong, but just existing . . . feelings just are." (M. S. Schiering 1972)

Defining Social Experiences: Model's First Interior Component

Social Experiences are seen as the understandings one has about a variety of things. It could be the occurrence of going to a movie, watching television, or being on the computer surfing the internet or researching, as easily as it could be driving a car, riding a bicycle, or talking with family or friends. Social experiences are the shared, collective, societal occurrences that take place every day in varied settings. Most importantly, social experiences are seen as communication between those in a setting that provides interaction mostly through verbal discourse, but it could also be watching a ball game or playing in one, having dinner with another person or others, or just walking and talking, to say exactly, being with others and exchanging, perhaps, thoughts, ideas, opinions, judgments, and feelings.

Defining Beliefs and Values: Model's Second Interior Component

It should be noted that beginning beliefs and values start in the home as a result of what is modeled in that space. Then, these may change over time as new experiences are added to one's reflection points. In the book *Teaching and Learning: A Model for Academic and Social Cognition*, beliefs and values are defined as:

> "Beliefs are one's concept involving thinking and feelings as to whether something is true, untrue, good, bad, or even exists.
> "Values involve beliefs as to whether something is right or wrong, or the level of importance something has, which is based on one's experience." (M. S. Schiering 2013)

CLASSROOM, HOME, OR CHARACTER EDUCATION WORKSHOP ACTIVITY: CHARACTER DEVELOPMENT— DISCOVERING BELIEFS AND VALUES

Activity Purpose and Definition

Realizing individual's beliefs and values is the main objective/purpose of this interaction. The reason for that realization is so we may discover "who" we are at the core of our social thinking, as it's based on what one sees as representing himself and how important that is. An example might be not speaking when someone else is doing that and referring to that as a means of respect (see chapter 5 for more information on respect) or being polite. Then, values address what level of importance one attaches to the belief. For example, one might believe in having good health, and the value is of high importance.

How do I know you? How do I know what you think and feel? How do I know the "you" of you or the "me" of me? Why would I want to know the answers to these questions? Simplistically, by knowing the answer to these questions, one has a sense of belonging that develops in the classroom. A feeling that one is safe in the classroom environment may be possible, because the basis of what's important is shared. This author thinks that there needs to be an exchange of what one thinks and feels, as well as a realization of one's own thinking and feelings concerning what is held to be true or untrue, and the other words that describe beliefs in the preceding section. The same can be said in answer to the question, "What do you value?"

An important part of character education and its development is founded in this forthcoming explained activity, because it's designed to discover the beliefs and values of those gathered together. Most times in a classroom this topic is not addressed, because the curriculum or subject matter takes precedence over everything. The tests given to students and their doing well on them, reflecting on the teacher's ability to teach, are considered important. Knowing what gives one comfort or what he or she is concerned about is rarely shared, because the academics of a classroom take precedence over the social cognition of it.

With the importance of knowing one's students kept close at hand, this beliefs and values activity is designed to bring acknowledgment and realization of what is believed and valued by those in the assemblage. When a class gets to know each other, there is a bonding that occurs, and each person works toward a goal that promotes community and caring. Conversely, without knowing what one's students believe and/or value, the teacher would probably teach the subject in the same way to the same people in a particular time period. Before any classroom's students do well, one needs to know the social realities that join the group together or may separate them. By knowing what is believed and valued in a class, at any grade level, one hopes that the similarities will outweigh the differences, and the joining together for a common goal and interest areas will follow, as each person is concerned about the overall well-being of others.

Activity Directions

Separate the class into groups of four or five. Have the group select a leader and on paper have two columns. The left one is titled Beliefs and the right one Values. Have the group decide what goes where and mention that sometimes what one believes is also valued. An example might be belief in good health and valuing it, simultaneously.

When the lists are complete, have chart paper on the wall and have each group provide a representative to come and list the Beliefs and Values, as shared in their group. Then, examining these beliefs and values after reading them aloud, the whole class shares, regarding comparing and contrasting these listed beliefs and values. The class should discover that there are more similarities than differences when it comes to what those assembled believe and value.

Example of Beliefs and Values Listing

The combined list of two workshops for character development at Molloy College yielded the following:

> *Beliefs:* Family, Being polite, God, Education, Technology, Good health, Exercise, Spirituality, Money, Success, Relationships, Positive thinking, The golden rule, Fairness, Kindness, Caring, Compassion, Self-acceptance, Moral behavior, Good grades, Democracy, Freedom, The right to assemble, Have a free press, and Concern for oneself and understanding of others, Don't interrupt, Be an active listener, Accepting, decision-making, and Open-mindedness.
>
> *Values:* All of the items mentioned in Beliefs were valued with one or two stars being put next to the most important ones. Interestingly, "technology" was qualified as finding some forms of its being more important than others. And, Social Media networks were seen as a bonus and a detriment to society and social experiences. Chocolate was put as a value, good health, designer clothes, time alone, playing or watching baseball or a particular sport, friends, college, time with others, dancing, food, clothing, shelter, cell phones, video games and particular apps, as well as conversations with parent(s) being valued.

IN-CLASS REACTION TO BELIEF AND VALUES ACTIVITY

As for a class, members valuing chocolate and friendships had two stars put by each one. Of greatest importance of the values were good health, food, clothing, and shelter. Each of these was considered to be of formidable importance, and the list continued with power, good nutrition, the color green, prayer, good teeth, love of a significant other, and the availability of jobs with good pay and time to relax. Additional importance was put on one's being responsible, accepting oneself, being nice to others, ability to make decisions, flexibility, kindness, and open-mindedness.

When asked about what the group thought children in the age range of five to twelve would value, the class stated that perhaps "play dates, going to Disney World, video games, fast-food, pizza, love, good grades in school, friendships, nice parents, Netflix, being involved in sports, or some after-school extra-curricular activity program, and staying up late. These would be of importance, based on one's experiences.

Following the listing of these items on the chart paper on the wall, the class began a discussion on beliefs and values that lasted over an hour as comparisons were made to perceived cultural influences and politics impacting beliefs and values.

CLASSROOM, HOME, OR CHARACTER EDUCATION WORKSHOP ACTIVITY: KNOWING ABOUT YOURSELF AND OTHERS THROUGH DAILY EXPERIENCES

Preface for Activity

In the beginning of this chapter and then again a few pages later, the idea of daily experiences shaping the "you" of you was suggested. The following activity is for reflection and sharing. It may be done at any grade level or in any setting such as a workplace or social gathering.

Activity Purpose

Overall, the following exercise is designed to bring about awareness of self and others, perhaps even a comparison and contrast and finding similarities and/or differences of experiences. Frankly, whenever this activity has been incorporated into a workshop, the *observable result* is that those having a partner or are in a small group discover that there are likenesses more so than differences. Its overall focus is to use meta-cognitive processes of recalling and reflection and thereby bring about a reference to times in your life that formed your present personality. Or, it may be the sharing of the activity participants that helps to define a distinctiveness that refers to character and its development as a result of character education.

An example was given in chapter 2 with the bicycle story. That was an experience that shaped that individual's viewpoint on the ability to "let go." Other experiences we have and share help to create a bond within the environment chosen for sharing. This sharing, which provides an opportunity to have conversations "with" others, frequently creates a bond and, in so doing, builds a sense of oneness and community within that setting. Why? The answer is because you have shared part of yourself with another by communicating meaningfully.

This activity relies on relating different time periods in one's life. These are explained as key points for realizing that remembering these times in our life is because the emotional experience was significant enough to cause memory to ensue. A sharing of these times is done in partnerships and then, at the discretion of the character education deliverer of information, whole-group/class formats.

Activity Directions

You are asked to lead and be part of a sharing of thoughts and/or feelings you have had during the following 1–5 time periods. You may select one or several of these. The objective of the activity is to share and converse with another person or persons. Please note that the early years when you were very little, such as being a baby or toddler, might not be recalled but told to you by an older sibling or parent, or a witness to your behavior that helped form the "you" of you. Our memories are sometimes interconnected with others who were observing us. Their perception later impacts our present-time character through our actions or perceived earlier behaviors.

Time Periods:

1. Being a baby
2. Toddler years
3. School years at the elementary level or later
4. Chores and jobs/occupation desired or experienced
5. Community participation

Follow-up: Realizing, as stated earlier, we are each our experiential past, we come to have memories of *experiences that shaped our life and formed our beliefs and values mentioned in the first activity* of this chapter. The significance of the situation when it occurred was so powerful that it was carried forward and assisted us/one in making decisions. In a partnership or small-group sharing, you are asked to connect the daily experiences or at least one of these that helped you, in your opinion, form a particular belief or value.

In chapter 2, there were two examples of beliefs that followed significant events during one's childhood and then early twenties. The beliefs were about a desire to hold on to others, as opposed to "letting go," and then for the second realization, allowing for time with friends.

This is the time to connect the first activity with the second one in this chapter. Locate at least one emotional experience that was so significant for you, and share how this formed a belief or value that you presently have. You may use the time periods at the start of this daily experience activity or select something that happened more recently. The choice is yours, but the objective is to get to know one another on a social literacy or experience level.

JOURNAL AND/OR DISCUSSION QUESTIONS

1. What are the components of the social cognition learning model?
2. What is the definition of beliefs and values?
3. What's the cognitive collective?
4. What is the difference between thoughts and feelings?
5. How do social experiences differ from academic ones?
6. What do you suppose were the objectives of the chapter's two activities?
7. How did it feel to share your feelings with a partner?

Chapter 4

She Had Cooties: A Bullying Incident

CHAPTER OVERVIEW

What comes before addressing character education and development is the need for these. Chapter 1 dealt with that concept. This chapter deals with a situation that is the opposite of being a person of good character. It's a chapter for recognizing that bullying, harassment, discrimination, and prejudice have real effects and affects on an individual experiencing these disquieting behaviors. The chapter also explains how one may be a "change agent" and bring others to practice being a person of good character in a society that all too often centers on failures of persons, negativity, and finding a reason not to like another, or for that matter oneself.

After a true story where the opposite of good character traits was exhibited toward an eight-year-old girl, the topic of "What's wrong with you?" is given attention. An activity addressing "What's right with you?," as opposed to "What's wrong with you?," is provided with activity preface, activity purpose, and activity directions. A few quotes from the booklet *Be-Good-to-Yourself Therapy* (Hartman 1987) are provided. The chapter ends with "Journal and/or Discussion Questions."

SOCIAL SETTING: UNATTRACTIVE BEHAVIORS

What do you think of when reading the title of this particular section? Perhaps a lot of ugly images come to mind. Answers this author got from third graders were: "You must mean like someone spitting, or picking their nose." There was agreement regarding these being rather disgusting behaviors. But, the author referenced ones occurring all around us, at places where people of all ages gather, across our country and worldwide, according to multimedia reports.

For example, disgusting behaviors may include *bullying* in and around schools. This has become commonplace along with picking on someone by *harassing*, *discriminating* against individuals, due to their being from a different religion, race, age, gender, ethnic group, size, socioeconomic level, and the list continues. The same may be said for *prejudice*, although that seems to have its origins in family behaviors where this conduct has previously been exhibited and modeled. What do you consider disgusting or unattractive behavior in a social setting?

One Reason for Unattractive Behaviors

There may be a multitude of reasons for the exhibition of "unattractive behaviors." However, aside from family influence, there are peer pressure, sense of being a failure, or desire to be better than another. Then again, perhaps there's desire to be a member of a group. When asking children in a fifth-grade class what they'd do to be in a group or accepted by classmates, many responded in written format with one word and that was, "anything." When asking a group of teacher candidates what they thought children at the elementary, middle, and high schools' levels would do to be accepted in a group, they responded, collectively, with the word, "anything." Interesting that the age difference was ten to fifteen years, but the answer was the same.

While these two places and/or groups of people yielded the same answer, it's surely not the only one. There may be many reasons. Using the socio-centricity concept of Wilber (2000), one may link these behaviors to group membership. Million (2010) explains that "socio-centricity is the idea that people belong to a group, and the group defines what is acceptable and what is permitted behavior in order to be a member of the group."

This author explains that there are lots of groups, and some are defined by culture, while others by the rules of social engagement or abilities to, let's say, play a musical instrument or be part of a sports team in baseball, golf, swimming, technology-based, and so forth. Are these groups' examples, by their titles, of unattractive behaviors? Probably not! However, the idea of belonging to a group that has antisocial behaviors is not uncommon if one is willing to conform to the rules of the group for acceptance.

Ask yourself what are the rules for the groups to which you belong? Where are the groups based—in the community, at a school, faith path–oriented, sports-minded, video games, technology-centered, political preference or, something else? What would you do to remain a member of the group? Are you a conformist or nonconformist or does this depend on the situation?

Now, you're asked to think about children, what would those in an age group five to twelve, thirteen to eighteen, nineteen to thirty, thirty to forties, fifties and sixties, or beyond that do to be part of a group? Each age may have different criteria for the desire to be in a social setting of those with similar interests. However, in all likelihood, it's not the age level so much as desire to have a sense of belonging with others that serves as a determining factor for group membership.

College Classroom Question

Recently, a group of freshmen students in children's literature in a downstate New York class was asked why no one was wearing a speedo or bikini swimsuit. After the laughter died down, the answers came forward that this wasn't an acceptable attire for a college classroom and besides it was January and the temperatures were quite low. The ultimate answer focused on how this type of dress was not accepted by college students as being appropriate more so than the cold temperatures.

A look around the room found students realizing other conformities that identified them as college students of a particular age. One was their overall style of dress, another was women's and men's hair length, makeup on females, and college courses being taken. Note that each was applicable for individuals. The idea of how the desks were arranged or what was being addressed, subject-wise, was not part of their membership rules.

Doing well in their studies was a group membership requirement. Subsequently, with these examples, it can be seen that even if a group has allowed for behaviors of a negative nature, these are accepted as part of the group membership and, if not agreed upon, then membership isn't permitted. Children will conform to being part of a group as much as an adult will.

Adult Groups

What constitutes an adult group's areas of commonality and reasons for forming a group? Of course, the first thing that comes to mind is their age. Then, some of these groups are formed in accordance with spiritual belief concepts and others by the neighborhood in which one lives. Then again, a group may form based on educational experiences, job titles, or places of employment. Another popular joining point is by technology savvy, vacation preferences, type of house or living quarters, style of speech, knowledge of historical events, sport preferences for watching or participating, and recreational interests such as card playing. There are all sorts of ways people differentiate themselves and form groups that are comfortable because of likenesses.

Is it possible for adults to belong to a group or multiple groups? Yes, it is. Is it possible to have adults in a group that has bullying, harassment, discrimination, or prejudices? In all likelihood, the answer to that question would be, "Yes." This is evidenced with willingness to be negative, make sarcastic statements, and join in rhetoric that causes divisiveness in social settings.

You are invited to ask yourself about where you feel comfortable. What are some groups to which you belong, and what are the rules of behavior to which you attest? When you think about that, those of you who are reading this book, you will know about yourself and your willingness to address the topic of being a *change agent* if it's seen to be necessary for harmony. That means going against the present norm or group qualifications, if applicable, with promoting positive behaviors and simply living/modeling character education components. While doing that, you might be asking others you are with to do the same, mainly to avoid sarcasm, mockery, derision, scorn, disdain, and cynicism.

THE BULLY STORY: COOTIES

This story begins with an understanding that it's about the aforementioned negative behaviors exhibited by a few children who belonged in a third-grade group when the main character was eight years old. She was a member in this same class, but sociocentricity had divided the overall class into separate groupings . . . some community-minded and some not. The fact that the child, main character, ran home to seek help and got it is what changed the way many later behaved when in her presence. Mind you, this was done through a bit of trickery, but the end result altered some individual's behaviors, possibly forever. The once fractured third-grade class became a whole group that was able to accept one another.

The setting is in upstate New York outside an elementary school. The storyteller and the one who had the experience in this narrative is this book's author, and her main mood was, at first, calm. Then it changed to being fearful and genuinely scared. Finally, the moods were relief and confidence. While the moods were modified because of the different incidents that were happening, the main character would have preferred staying with the relaxed one.

"It was a spring day. School had been dismissed, and I was outside looking for fossils. We had been studying dinosaurs and fossils for about a week in my third-grade class, and I figured if I could find one, my family would be rich. We'd be rich because we'd take the fossil to the museum in our town and we'd sell it there for a fortune."

At this juncture, the storyteller explains that while she knew finding a fossil in or on the school's playground was unlikely, she wanted to "have a look." She further explained that bringing home a fossil would be "chill" and she'd get a lot of attention. Possibly this would be more attention than her older brother got and that'd be "terrific."

The storyteller continued, "I got up from digging in the grass where the only thing I'd found was dirt. I stood there for a few minutes and wondered if I should be walking home. Realizing that everyone had gone and I was not supposed to walk home alone, I noticed a few classmates coming my way. There were two girls and two boys; Billy, Mary, Tom, and Jackie (not their real names). Maybe they'd walk home with me.

"There was no 'Hi.' They just immediately asked what I was doing and I was hesitant to reply. In the space where I was formulating an answer they said I looked disgusting . . . really disgusting. 'Whew,' they remarked, as they held their noses and backed away from me. I wondered why they were saying this, but I didn't need to wait too long. One of them said, 'You have Cooties.'"

"'I have what?' Cooties, was repeated, as I questioned what those were. The reply came quickly with how these things were bugs so small that few, if any, could see them because they were imaginary germs or disease that could be transmitted by touching an infected person. In fact, for most people, such as me, they were invisible. But Mary, Billy, Tom, and Jackie could easily see them and evidently I was covered with them. They started pushing at me, or more likely, as I recall, gestured like they were pushing me away. This gesture was because they weren't sure if they touched me what would happen. Would there be Cootie transfer? They repeated how disgusting I was and how these 'bugs' were all over me and I'd better get home or go somewhere that I couldn't spread these to others.

"I ran home, hysterically crying. I burst through the door of my house and taking two steps at a time, I ran up the stairs still sobbing. My mom heard me come through the door, felt me flash by, and yelled up the stairs asking about what was happening. I told her 'nothing' but yelled back to not follow me or come to my room. I sat on my bed and cried and cried and cried. My mom yelled up the stairs a few times, but didn't come up there, as I recall.

"A short time later, when one would think my tears would have stopped, my dad came home. Evidently my mom told him I was in my room and upset about something and had ordered her not to come upstairs. My dad yelled from the first floor and asked what was happening. He asked me several times. I yelled back that nothing was going on and not to come upstairs. He could hear me crying and in a stern voice demanded that I come downstairs or he'd be forced to come upstairs and see what was going on with me. I responded with how he'd better not come upstairs and my behavior was such that he said my first name and middle one too. He did this most sternly and that told me that I'd better get downstairs . . . *right now!*

"I complied with his demand, although reluctantly. I stood in front of him in the living room, shoulders shuddering and a new batch of tears streaming down my face. I told him with my shaky voice that I had Cooties and that meant a bunch of them; not one 'Coot' but many. 'Hmm', was his reply with a wry smile on his face. He said he'd have to examine me further and checked my hair. He instructed me to put my arms straight out to my sides and he checked them with a visual perusal. He had me remove my shoes and socks as he looked between my toes, before proclaiming 'You've no Cooties.'

"I could feel my heart pounding as I gasped and asked him how he knew this because these Cooties were invisible. 'Not to me,' he replied. 'Why aren't they invisible to you, Daddy?' And this is where he was, reflectively speaking, a genius. He pulled from his pocket his driver's license and showed it to me. Never having seen this paper before and actually not even being able to read very well, I heard him state emphatically, pointing to this paper, 'See this, I am an official Cootie Inspector.'

"I gasped, 'A Cootie Inspector?' You're a 'Cootie Inspector,' I asked him doubtfully. He replied in the affirmative and showed me where it had written, 'New York State,' and then showed me his printed name and signature. This happened in a flash of time before he asked me who had told me I had Cooties. I gave him the names. My dad told me to go to school the next day and tell these children that he is an official 'Cootie Inspector'. Additionally, he told me that they're probably those who have Cooties and he would be going to their house and be checking them out to see if they had Cooties. This would happen *if* they didn't leave me alone.

"The next day I went to school and Billy, Mary, Tom, and Jackie formed sort of a circle around me and started their bullying again. I told them exactly what my dad told me to say and interestingly they backed off and almost instantly became friendly, telling me they were just fooling around. It was an amazing thing, and I not only stopped these children bullying me (or fear of my dad did), but over a short period of time, leaving other kids alone also was evidenced.

"My dad's cleverness saved me, no doubt about that. But, what if there is no one to save a bullied child or adult that is afraid to speak out for fear of the unknown or being rejected by others? My answer is start being a person who promotes being one of good character, one who promotes the positive in self and others. I have found that oftentimes it only takes one person to make a difference. If you're the teacher then you may well be that person by emphasizing what's 'right' with your students as opposed to what's wrong. It would serve one well to do the same thing for him/herself, as '*Putting yourself down serves no purpose*" (M. S. Schiering 2000–present; 2013).

ADDRESSING WHAT'S "RIGHT" WITH ME AND/OR YOU

How many times do you suppose you've said to yourself one of these statements: "What's wrong with me? What were you thinking? Why did you do that? What's wrong with you? Why did you say that?"

In this author's opinion, our society is accustomed to put-down type statements, finding and emphasizing what's wrong with one's -self or others. Let me ask you how many times you've heard someone say, "What's right with you?" I hesitate to say that most frequently others are more than willing to tell you what's wrong with you or that one will chastise himself or herself on a regular basis. An example would be my husband driving the car to take us to a friend's house. He is supposed to turn left at the stoplight, but instead doesn't make the turn. Almost immediately I say, "What's wrong with you? Why didn't you make that turn?"

My husband's response might be that he'd forgotten to make the turn, but would turn left at the next street and then left at the following one and left again to our friend's street, which would put us in the correct place with her house just a few houses down the block. "And it'll take us an additional three minutes to get there," I respond angrily. To what end was my telling or asking him what was wrong? Do you think my anger was worth the aggravation he felt or I did by yelling and questioning him? Yet, this is a common occurrence and one that is typical. What's wrong with you? What about saying what's right?

NEGATIVE SUPPOSITION AND ACCEPTING COMPLIMENTS

How often do you suppose that we, as adults, teens, children, or a general society, take on the ideas of others' telling us what's right with us? Are we more geared to listening for what's wrong? Take an everyday situation. Let's say ten people say something like, "Whoa, nice jacket" and one person says, "What's with the jacket?" Which comment do you think of all day, the ten that praised you or the one who wasn't giving a put-down but asking you a question about what you're wearing? Needless to say, most times it's the latter. That one person who doesn't even make a negative statement, but doesn't compliment either is taken as negativity and focused on all day . . . maybe longer than that.

Let's say this happens. "Wow, nice jacket" comes from nine people and in the middle of those nine one says, "Now that's an ugly jacket!" This time you're not being asked a question about the jacket, but told boldly that it's not attractive. Do you question that person's opinion or think about what's so ugly about it? Do you center your attention on those who thought the jacket looked great and thank them for their comment? Chances are you look at the negative and may not even acknowledge the compliment statements.

GIVING AND RECEIVING COMPLIMENTS

The other day it was overheard in a classroom that one fourth-grade girl was telling her friend how much fun she'd had at the amusement park with this girl's family just a month ago. The recipient of the compliment shrugged it off with a "Did you see Kerri there too?" No acknowledgment of the going to the amusement park was noted. Giving and receiving compliments are a forerunner for being a change agent and something that, in teaching character development, is good to address.

Instead of one's ignoring the compliment, character education explains, a simple "Thank you" would suffice. Or, in the amusement park scenario, the recipient of the compliment should not triangulate to a different topic, but say something like, "Yes, it was fun." Saying that reinforces the good feeling and the memory of the amusement park. (Of course, it should be understood that the compliment given was done so to understand that the two fourth graders at the amusement park did have a good time.)

Sometimes compliment training is called for, as the majority of people don't see/hear compliments, as they're geared more to put-down statements. When the put-down isn't there, a person wonders if the compliment is made because the person giving the compliment wants something in return. Seriously! Reading that seems ridiculous, but there it is, a concern for being asked to do something or give something instead of just acknowledging the compliment and saying "Thank you."

WORKSHOP EXAMPLE OF "WRONG VERSUS RIGHT"

A professor conducting a character education workshop had spoken previously with a teacher candidate in the workshop about whether she'd volunteer to be the recipient of put-down statements at some point during the class. These would involve the professor's reaction to her moving slowly when asked to move to a seat in the front of the room. The professor explained that initially the class would not know this was a role-play, as it was designed to see their reaction to it. The teacher candidate was asked to either not respond to the professor and/or try to make an excuse as to why she'd moved so slowly. She volunteered most willingly, and when the time came, the dialogue and action went like this:

1. *Professor:* (There is an empty chair beside the teacher. Sandy comes forward, empty-handed, and sits down.) "Sandy, please come from the back of the room where you're sitting and take this chair beside me." *Professor:* (Raising her voice and speaking to Sandy) "Why did you move so slowly and sit down so awkwardly?"
2. *Professor:* "Are you listening to me? Why did you move so slowly? What's *wrong* with you? Clearly there is something *wrong* . . . something is the matter with you for you to just saunter over here and you seemed reluctant to sit in the chair. Are you listening to me?"

3. *Sandy:* "Umm."
4. *Professor:* "Was that an answer? Did you really try to formulate a sentence, or are you mocking me? What's *wrong* with you; don't you know I'm the one who signs the paper to give the okay for you having taken this course? Really, there's something *wrong* with you!"
5. *Sandy:* (Sandy is visibly shaking by being bullied, harassed, and shamed by the professor.)
6. *Workshop Attendees:* The workshop attendees started out laughing awkwardly and then became silent when the professor raised her voice and seemed truly annoyed. The professor, at break time, was told that most attendees were thinking that if this is what a character education workshop is like then they didn't want to continue the workshop.
7. *Professor Explanation:* The professor then smiled at Sandy and the others there. She explained that there was nothing wrong with Sandy, but she served as an example of how one reacts when being told there is something "wrong" with him/her. Hurt feelings, confusion, and wanting to escape the situation follow. The professor then said, "There's nothing 'wrong' with Sandy. In fact she was extremely fantastic in this role-play. If anything, Sandy played the scenario very well. She played the role 'right'. Please do applaud her now."
8. *Attendees:* (The attendees applauded Sandy, and the assemblage went on to engage in some conversation with one another about the role-play and their responses to it at the beginning, middle, and end parts.)

This scenario was the lead-in to an activity about recognizing *What's Right with You*.

CLASSROOM, HOME, OR CHARACTER EDUCATION WORKSHOP ACTIVITY: WHAT'S RIGHT WITH YOU?

Activity Preface

Let me begin this activity by relating that for a long time this character-guiding teacher found herself getting up in the morning and doing self-talk that was negative. She might say that she had so much to do that day and it was all going to go badly. Or, she'd question what she was wearing and say that she had nothing decent to wear. These were, as seen now, defeating statements. They had nothing to do with anything but making her feel bad about herself. About fifteen years ago she changed that morning statement to one where she stood in front of the bedroom mirror and said, rather loudly, "You are drop-dead gorgeous, and you're going to have a great day."

Interestingly, whenever a classroom full of students is told what she says, they laugh. "Why are you doing that," she questions. "Do you think I am not drop-dead gorgeous, or do you think I'm not going to have a great day?" To this moment, that question has never been answered.

Activity Purpose

The "drop-dead gorgeous" scenario begins an activity that deals with two components that serve as the focus of this interaction. The first is to realize that there are things about us that are good and as society may use the word, "right." The second idea is to share that with another to establish a sense of fellowship and then share through texting or sending an e-mail or note to someone that establishes letting that person know he or she is of value to you. What's *right* with the one you're writing is emphasized.

Activity Directions

1. Forerunner: Turn to the person next to you and tell him or her one thing that is right about *you*. You might say that you are thoughtful, caring, considerate, generous, or understanding. The idea is to practice recognizing something right or good about you and the way you conduct yourself.
2. Now, if you're in a classroom where there is no access to cell phones or e-mail, ask those in the room to write down something right about someone they know in the class and take this to that person for sharing. If they prefer to write to someone not in the class, then they're to do that and share their writing later that day.

   However, if you're in a place where there are adults or adolescents who have cell phones, ask them to text someone something that's *right* about that person. Please be aware that you first need to say that you're being instructed to do this, because you're in a character education workshop or have been instructed to do this. Be aware and tell those texting that the usual responses include: "What do you want? What did I do wrong now? Yeah, right, and what got into your brain?"
3. The reason for predominately negative responses to receiving a text stating what's right about him or her is because of the recipient's being surprised with such a positive. It's partially the unexpectedness. Most texts are about innocuous things such as instructions for something, or asking how one is, or what he or she is doing, or things of a mundane nature. One does not expect an "I love you" or "I was so impressed with what you did or said or this is what's great about you" message.

   But, when this activity is repeated, when one writes several people about what's right with that person they're sharing the concept of uplifting statements, then the response might be to return the compliment. This author, using this activity in workshops on character education has found that it takes about twenty minutes to have the attendees get positive feedback in a return text message.

4. Now imagine that you did this "What's right with you" texting every day. How long would it take to establish a *pattern of behavior* that is positive-based? How long till the text message recipient gives this a try with you or others? You won't know the answer until you try. Be a change agent and start this practice of saying to yourself something that's right with you and then texting something "right" with another. Try it. You'll see it works. *Spread the idea of "What's Right with You."*

LIFT YOURSELF *UP*

In a little booklet by Cherry Hartman (1987) there are thirty-seven ideas for being positive with yourself. The introduction for this writing asks if you feel bad and if you express anger, and if you select attitudes that drag you down. The question of whether you're ashamed of your feelings as well as whether you experience guilt when you put your own needs before those for others is asked. The book was designed, the author states, to help overcome the distorted options that keep one from living fully.

Some of these statements for being good to yourself include: "Trust yourself; you know what you want and need; you can't be anything for someone else unless you take care of yourself first; value your thinking; when someone loves you just accept and be glad; when you need help ask; Breathe."

JOURNAL AND/OR DISCUSSION QUESTIONS

1. What do you suppose are reasons for bullying, harassment, discrimination, and/or prejudice?
2. How do you think one may prevent the antisocial behaviors from happening?
3. What are the reasons for putting people down or making negative comments?
4. What was your impression of the Cootie story?
5. What is your response to the activity about "What's right with you?"
6. What could be your morning statement to yourself?

Section II

R-E-S-P-E-C-T: Realizations about Teaching Character Development

SECTION OVERVIEW

Chapters 5, 6, and 7 form a "section" of this book and are considered important for character education and development instruction. This is because these chapters address the six international traits of a person of good character. Chapter 5 begins with the character trait of being *respectful*. Specifically, chapters 6 and 7 address each of the remaining person-of-good-character traits. Each attribute addressed in the specified chapter is titled. Then, the definition is provided with anecdotes about where this trait was witnessed. Or, there may be a story about a time when the individual involved, personally, acted on this trait.

CHAPTER OVERVIEW

This chapter commences with a light review of the previous chapters and added material about how to address teaching character development. After that, there's a true story about a sixteen-year-old athlete that served as the impetus for a character development workshop. This was and still is, as the teenager's mother relates, a "life lesson" story. The story took place in 1999, and the workshop commenced in 2000 and continues to this day at Molloy College in Rockville Centre, New York.

An activity is provided with purpose and directions that addresses one's being respectful. This is accomplished by recording on a chart titled "A Person Who Is Respectful Is . . .," the behaviors associated with one's being respectful. Two questions are then asked, which are followed by the introduction of the six international traits of a person with good character.

55

Before the chapter ends with "Journal and/or Discussion Questions," a listing of Dewey's (1937) six areas of commonality between all cultures is provided by topic. The reactions to these six situations are given with the idea that these reactions bind us together as a world community. Mix these with the international traits of a person of good character and we have the total essence of character education by realizing that we share common social situations and experiences and have reactions to them that bring us together through *sharing with* one another.

A LIGHT REVIEW AND ADDED VIEW

Each of the previous chapters has had an activity to bring home the concepts presented in each chapter. These commenced with realizing that negative statements can cause hurt feelings that last three years to a lifetime. Then, activities involving getting acquainted, one's personal beliefs and values, daily experiences, and a few others provide support for the chapter's content dealing with how to teach character development.

The added viewpoint is a reiteration of the idea not to put yourself down but to give yourself lift-up statements. Additionally, modeling a person of good character is imperative in character education at any age/grade level. Don't expect people to do what you say unless you actively engage in being that type of person. Positivity is a must! While sarcasm may be a trend and a form of humor, realize it is usually hurtful to the recipient. Be an active listener.

There's one best time to apply the concepts in this book and that time is *now*!

A STORY ABOUT RESPECT

It was a spring day, and the professor was at home getting prepared for the next day's doctorate class at a university in the New York City area. Standing in the kitchen, she overheard her sixteen-year-old having a conversation about some activities he'd planned for the next day when she and her husband would be at work. The young man looked every bit the formidable football player and track star that he was. He was 250 pounds and slightly over six feet tall. Now a personable young man, he had been, until recently, a person good at sports but a failure in all of his academic endeavors. His mother asked him at dinner that night if he'd come to her college classroom the next day and speak about how he had changed his persona/character over the past year.

"Mom," he said emphatically, "I have plans for tomorrow." "Could you change them," his mother asked. Reluctantly he said he could, but would rather not. His mother asked him to think about this request and let her know later. As it turned out, he did change his plans, and his mother instructed him that he'd need to come to her class in attire that was not too casual, as he would want to make a good impression and the dress code is rather formal at the university. "Dress in nice pants and a collared shirt and be formidable when you present by walking forward and to the sides and making eye contact with the forty-five doctoral candidates." He smiled and said, "Yeah, sure."

On the ride to the university, the professor's son asked his mom what she wanted him to say to the class. "Oh my," his mother thought, "I really don't know because I really just wanted you out of the house." What she actually said was, "Talk about how you failed in school up until this year. Tell the students that your attitude about learning has dramatically changed." He replied, "Seriously, that's what you want me to tell them?"

"Yes, it's a reality check," she responded and continued with, "How are they going to know about the thoughts and feelings of teenagers unless someone comes forward and shares them? You can be enlightening for them as they go into their teaching and/or administrative education profession."

Coming into the university classroom, the high school student noticed there were approximately forty-five female doctoral candidates ranging in age from twenty-three to fifty-five. He was a bit disgruntled, as he thought the whole class would be maybe seven years older than he. Nonetheless, he was introduced to the class, and he began a fifteen-minute presentation that was in the style of delivery that his mom had requested of him. He fully addressed, chronologically, what it was like to fail in school in the beginning years, give up on himself by grade three, and things being that way up until ninth grade. Being a failure and everyone's seeing that and taking it on, personally, but doing well at football and track, made him wonder why he couldn't achieve.

This was his presentation: "Since I was in first grade, maybe before that, I had trouble in school and concentrating on what the teacher said. I started failing tests and didn't do homework, certainly by second grade. Things stayed that way, but I got either a social pass or when sharing in the classroom I sounded bright. But, then came seventh grade and a bunch of teachers who were not too thrilled with me. I stayed back as I repeated the year. At this point I think I was considered an oddball. I could do well in sports, but not in much else."

"Although my parents praised me, assured me of my intelligence, and offered me money, trips, and/or special privileges for good grades, nothing seemed to help. Basically, I saw myself as a failure and believed I was a failure and accepted myself as a failure, except at sports."

"Of course, this impacted my social life, as I felt separated from my classmates. While good grades weren't everything, not having them sure kept me from being accepted or having people listen to me. Guess they thought I was a great athlete, but not too bright. I would say that I 'sort a' agreed. The one saving grace was being a football star. The cheerleaders thought I was pretty 'with it' and I got some attention there."

Opening the class to questions they might have following his formal presentation, one candidate asked, "What made your self-perception of being a failure change? After you refused to accept any of the 'rewards' offered you, what made the turn-around happen?"

The reply came quickly with, "My first success! Once I had one, I knew I could have two and three, or as many as I wanted. I just needed that first one to tell me I was okay. Actually, I had to be willing to challenge myself. What if I tried and failed? For a lot of years, I didn't want to know whether, if I tried, I'd succeed. My first success was in studying for a ninth-grade English test. I earned a grade of 100 percent. It was my first real academic achievement. I realized that one success could lead to another."

Another woman in the class who was in her mid-forties, asked how teachers could get teenagers to be respectful. The young man sauntered forward and stood very close to the woman. He answered with an assured tone in his voice. "How do you get us to be respectful to you teachers? Well, how do I give you something I don't have for myself?"

You could hear the class gasp, immediately and simultaneously.
The professor's son elaborated, "If you are asked for a pen and you have one, then you can give it to the one who asked for it. But, if you don't have a pen, you can't do that. If you do not have self-respect, then you cannot give respect to another. You can only give to someone that which you yourself first have for you. I'm not talking about objects, but character traits."

In the aftermath of this experience, a workshop was created for teaching character development to teacher candidates and student learners. This quasi-course, whether in a home or academic setting, in kindergarten through advanced-degree college classrooms, both nationally and internationally, has found attendees very responsive to the concept presented when the main character of this story was sixteen years old. They responded that way, as it makes perfect sense! Concept: "You can give to another only that which you first have for yourself" (S.D. Schiering 1999).

CLASSROOM, HOME, OR CHARACTER EDUCATION WORKSHOP ACTIVITY: R-E-S-P-E-C-T

Activity Purpose

The main reason for this activity is to put participants in touch with what they think being "respectful" to others might entail. If one knows what showing or being respectful is to one's self and others, then it's something that can be acted upon in social settings.

Activity Directions

You need a piece of paper and/or chart paper on the wall, depending on how many are involved in this activity. Picture yourself seated in a group or with a partner or alone. It really doesn't matter, as this activity can be done in any type of configuration. If you are alone you may want to phone a friend and get some input to complete a chart on the topic of being respectful.

On teacher-provided chart paper, we're placing words/terms/actions that mean respect is being shown or demonstrated in word or deed to others. This list is configured following some reflection. The idea is to put words and/or actions you consider to be associated with a person being respectful. These could be words said or actions taken when socializing. Just the main word is necessary for this listing. An example would be "A person who is respectful is caring." The word "caring" would be placed on the paper or chart. Take it from there, and see if some of your responses or those of others agreed with the ones in the following list.

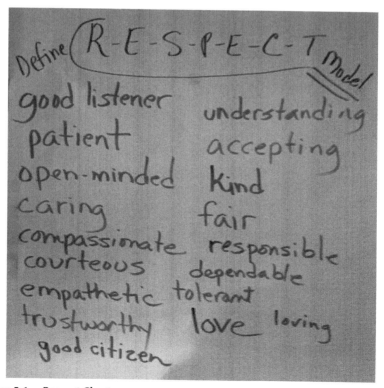

Figure 5.1. Respect Chart

Looking at the list there may be as many as twenty-one words listed. Ask the following questions:

1. Are you each of these (say each word on the list aloud: *respectful, caring, fair, trustworthy, responsible,* a *good citizen, and so forth*) to everyone you meet every day? Why or why not?
2. Are you each of these (say each listed word aloud) to yourself each day? Why or why not?

SIX INTERNATIONAL TRAITS OF BEING A PERSON OF GOOD CHARACTER

The six characteristics of being a person of good character include one's being *respectful, caring, fair, trustworthy, responsible,* and a *good citizen.* These traits, for this book, were originally constructed by a group consensus of educators in the Mount Morris Central School District in New York State. Schiering later used these in her workshop on preventing school violence and noted these same six behavioral actions placed on signs in hallways in schools she visited in Europe and South America.

Often one of these traits is exhibited, and then other times many are evidenced in one act by another or others, or oneself. Together, these six traits constitute *a good citizen.* In the chapters that follow, one to three of these character traits serve as the topic of the chapter. A definition of the behavior is given, and then an anecdote is provided for exemplifying when this character trait was either witnessed or practiced by the one doing the writing.

Giving preventing school violence workshops and, simultaneously, teaching graduate and undergraduate classes at the college level, this author had the opportunity to have teacher candidates contribute to this book. However, friends from childhood, teachers worked with over the span of more than forty years, student learners, and sometimes acquaintances share about the positivity they exhibited or witnessed concerning the six behaviors. For this chapter, the good character trait of "respect" has been selected for exemplification.

DEFINITION OF RESPECT

"Being respectful" means demonstrating to oneself and others, in thoughts and actions, courtesy, politeness, tolerance, compassion, open-mindedness, consideration, acceptance of individual differences, and appreciation.

Example of Being Respectful

Tim Ryley (2007/2017), a husband and dad of three girls, is an adjunct instructor at Molloy College in the Royal English Department. He also has assisted in the Preventing School Violence Program; Project SAVE (2008–present) at Molloy College. For the past nineteen years, he teaches tenth-grade English at Baldwin Senior High School in Long Island, NY. He writes: "At the risk of sounding clichéd, one of the most rewarding moments in a teacher's life is when he/she witnesses how students grow outside of the classroom. Over the course of my career, there is one event that for me clarified the qualities of a person's being respectful. In addition, there was caring and good citizenship.

"The event in question occurred about ten years ago (2007). As per our contract, the teachers at my school were required to fulfill a 'duty period.' During that year, my duty period was the 'Commons,' which is a large, open area adjacent to the cafeterias. My duties usually consisted in writing passes for students to go to either the library or the guidance office, as well as helping the security guards keep the students in the cafeterias until the bell rang to end the period. Over the course of the year, I got to know many students. Two stand out in my memory: 'Beth,' a junior or senior, kind-hearted girl who always greeted me warmly, and 'Bill,' a sophomore student with Asperger Syndrome.

"One of 'Bill's' obsessions was with 'coins.' He would always stop to pick one up, if he saw it in his path. Unfortunately, this made him a target for the cruelty of his peers. Often, they would throw coins at him, just to see him scramble to get them. The more coins they threw, the bigger the laugh. I would reprimand them for this, and they would promise not to do it again, responding with a half-hearted, 'Yeah, ok . . . sure thing.' I even brought it to the attention of the administration, who also spoke with these bullying persons. They would stop, but only for a little while.

"This changed one day when 'Beth' intervened. I remember the time well. It was mid-spring; most students were going out for lunch, as the weather was nice. The Commons was very busy. 'Bill' was walking across the Commons, making his way to the other side of the school. Students began throwing coins, howling with laughter as 'Bill' dove to scoop them up. This was when 'Beth' took action. She stood up, and 'called out' the student who had started the ridiculing.

"How dare you! How dare you make fun of Bill! Who do you think you are? Do you think that's funny? What's with you?' The young man whom she confronted had some 'choice words' for her in response, but she stood her ground, calling him out for his negative behavior. He made a motion to hit her, but was held back by his girlfriend. In addition, 'Beth's' action silenced the young man's followers; they shrank back from the spectacle they had created, shamed at being confronted for their cruelty.

"During this time I had alerted both the security guards and the administration. They quickly took action. The students who were bullying 'Bill' were disciplined for their actions. 'Beth' was commended for her actions. She told us that she could not stand what they were doing to 'Bill,' as it really bothered her that a fellow student with a disability was being held up for mockery.

"In short order, the teasing ceased.

"This event had a significant effect on me. First, as I mentioned before, it was refreshing to see a student 'grow' and demonstrate this outside of the classroom. We can teach our students algebra and trigonometry, we can teach them how to identify literary devices, and, we can teach them about the physical history of our planet. We can relish in watching the 'light bulb' go on over their heads when they make the important content-specific connections, but *the most gratifying moments come when we see them grow as people*. I was proud of Beth, as she stood up for someone when others would not. In this way, she demonstrated not just being respectful with accepting of Bill's individual differences, but also contributed to the well-being of this child and hence our school community.

"In addition, I think that Beth demonstrated the quality of being respectful, in that she did not allow the abuse and mistreatment of a fellow student to continue. I think that I will always reflect on Beth's actions. And, I will continue to be proud of her for being a person of good character."

Reflection on Beth's actions: Caring was shown when she cared for someone who was being made fun of for being different (bullied). She demonstrated compassion by caring enough not to be a bystander. Finally, Beth demonstrated the quality of being a *good citizen*, as she protected someone who had no one to speak on his behalf.

DEWEY'S SIX AREAS OF INTRA-INTER-CULTURAL SOCIAL EXPERIENCES FOR CHARACTER DEVELOPMENT

In 1937, educator John Dewey addressed six life experiences that all cultures' reactions to were similar. In doing thus he established a world community that could be easily envisioned with regard to these following life experiences. These six areas are: birth, death, success, failure, tradition, and love. Now, if one thinks about these, then it's rather obvious to see that reactions to these events are quite similar or even the same wherever one may reside. The following is the result of reactions that individuals from varied age groups had when presented with these common social realities:

1. Birth or knowledge of new life is responded to with joy, happiness, excitement, and generally feeling emotionally good or uplifted. The examples for birth were not only limited to human beings but also to a puppy, kitten, varied animals, and even seeing new sprouts on a plant.
2. Death or the passing of someone or the idea of a living thing no longer existing in this physical realm was met with sadness. Many people remarked that if the one passing was ill, that there was gladness or relief

about there being no more suffering. Still, there was an overall melancholy or sorrow related to the passing and no longer being in one's line of vision.

3. Success was considered first to be monetary-related and then there was success of having a good relationship, or doing well on tests, or good health and a myriad of other things that come to one's mind when thinking of being successful. The common reaction was that of well-being.

4. Failure was addressed first as not doing well on assessments and then expanded to job, having friends, and life in general. Specific areas of importance to particular individuals were added, but the reactions to failure were shame, disappointment, hopelessness, and despair.

5. Tradition was seen as celebration of holidays with family and/or friends. Different traditions for different cultures were noted with Thanksgiving being a forerunner in the United States. Birthdays were seen as a celebratory tradition and the reaction to observance of traditions connoted as times of gathering together to celebrate were a sense of happiness, contentment, delight, exhilaration, cheerfulness, and pleasure being observed.

6. Love was considered as the love of another individual, pet, friend, child, or parent. The response to love was a sense of satisfaction, joy, bliss, and contentment.

Ask yourself or those you are with when you're together for their reaction to these six common experiences from all cultures. Are you in agreement, and, if so, why do you think that is the case? If you're not in agreement, why do you suppose that happened?

JOURNAL AND/OR DISCUSSION QUESTIONS

1. What was the topic of this chapter and how does it influence your life?
2. What was your opinion of the high school student's explaining how you need to have something before you can give it to another? Why did you think that?
3. What was your opinion of the example given for the character trait of "respect"?
4. What is something you witnessed or is directly involved in for being a person of good character through demonstrating "respect"?

Chapter 6

Caring: Fair: Responsible

CHAPTER OVERVIEW

First a definition is given regarding what it means to be "caring." This is followed with two examples before the character trait of "fair" is defined with two anecdotal accounts provided. Being "responsible" closes the chapter with a definition of this behavior and two stories addressing when it was evidenced. It is reiterated that often the character traits representative of being a person of good character are interwoven so finely that they're like a tapestry. It is difficult to separate one character trait or, so to speak, one strand of fabric from another. Certainly that is the case for the examples given in these ten pages. "Journal and/or Discussion Questions" conclude this chapter.

DEFINITION OF CARING/KIND

Being "caring" means demonstrating to oneself and others, in thoughts and actions compassion, unselfishness, consideration, and interest through kind acts. Generally, a caring person treats others the way he or she would want to be treated. This means being helpful to others, and not being mean, cruel, or insensitive to the feelings of others.

A caring/kind person may open a door for someone, visit an ailing relative or friend, offer comforting words when someone is sad, exhibit actions that are uplifting for one's spirit, and offer emotional sustenance. Caring might mean making a meal for someone in need of that, sharing a time or event, or offering protection from a bully. A caring person, it should be noted, is not limited by age, gender, ethnicity, or level of education. The following examples are from two different parts of the country, New York and Colorado. They involve witnessing an act of caring, and one might say "kindness" as well.

Five Examples of Caring

1. "In the fall two years ago when I observed a third-grade class for Phase Two of my Teacher Education program. One little girl in particular in this class exhibited a sense-of-caring and being kind that I have never seen so prevalent in a child, previously. A little boy in this class was struggling with a math problem on his worksheet and was getting extremely frustrated with himself. The little girl put her hand on his arm, smiled at him, and told him that it was "Okay." She then showed him a simple way to solve the problem, and this helped him so much that his 'frustration' seemed to evaporate. It was a quick exchange, but a precious moment I will never forget being fortunate enough to witness." (Panzarino 2015a)

2. The characters in this story are two of a friend's grandchildren. She explains, "Cadence was six years old, and you know her family lives in California. She was visiting at her cousin's home in Colorado during the summer of 2013 when she got upset and started crying. Clearly, she was very sad. Jacob, age three at the time, came over with his orange blanket and said, 'Take my orgee blankie, 'cause it's always happy'. In Jacob's mind, his cousin was upset, and he wanted to comfort her, so he offered his possession as he thought it gave him solace so it would do the same for her if she held it.

   "I was amazed by this act of compassion. I learned that there is no age limit on exhibiting unselfishness and compassion. I have wondered if this act of caring was intrinsic or did someone teach him to be this way. Pretty much, I decided that when someone is hurting and it's a relatable experience then there may well be a reaching out to help the person in pain or who's upset. I'll tell you this: I was very proud of my grandson and amazed by his actions as well." (Byrne 2013)

3. "I volunteered for a week with Habitat for Humanity in New Orleans. Throughout the week, I worked with other volunteers to build the foundation of a house. During my time volunteering, I met a woman that had lost her home during Hurricane Katrina in 2005. She was working with us for the week because, to live in a house that is built by Habitat for Humanity volunteers; the 'homeowner' has to complete a certain number of hours volunteering with the organization. I got to know her during that week, and my friends and I ate lunch with her every day. At some point during that week, a picture was taken of us that we kept. After the trip, we went our separate ways but kept in touch."

"The following spring, I returned to New Orleans and worked with a different service organization. I visited with the woman that I met the previous year during the trip, and I had the privilege of being invited into her new home that was built during that year. While I was visiting, I brought the picture that we took together, framed for her home. When I presented it to her, she began to cry. She said that she was never treated with more kindness and respect than she was during that time. 'I have never felt more validated and accepted as a human being in my life,' she said."

"Prior to her sharing, I did not know how touched she was from that experience. To me, meeting her and getting to know her was something that I wanted to do. I enjoyed meeting her very much, but I had no idea how much it meant to her. My experiences volunteering in New Orleans and meeting the people that I have has been a life-changing experience. I learned that you can never know the impact that you make on other people's lives and that kindness is one of the greatest gifts that you can give a person. It costs nothing to give, but to receive it is priceless." (Spotkov 2017)

4. "I was recently asked to reflect on my forty-six years as an educator and administrator, from elementary school to college. This was to be done in terms of my own use of positive character traits and those I witnessed over that time span. As a principal, I was determined that our students have the best education they could have. That included strong character traits of the teachers and all staff.

"One act of kindness, that I was thanked for numerous times, occurred when I would make 'good calls' to the home of some of my students. All too often when the principal calls home, its purpose is to deliver a negative message. Consequently, most parents do not like to hear, 'The principal would like to speak to you.' I decided that I would not always be a part of that negativity. Thus, I began closely observing the students as they arrived, walked about the building, or were being dismissed from school. Lo and behold, I began to see some students doing nice things for other students. One day I observed a fifth-grade girl who was not well liked by her peers. She was helping a first grader who had lost her glasses and was really upset. The older student went with her through the hall and lunch room till she found the glasses. All the while she was telling the youngster not to worry.

"I decided personally to call the parent. The first reaction was, 'Oh no, what did she do?' When I explained the incident to the mother, she thanked me profusely. About ten minutes later I received a call from the father at his place of work, and he was telling me how happy I had made him and his wife feel. But, there's more to the story. A little while later in that day, I received a call from Florida from the grandmother who was thrilled that I would take the time to call her daughter with 'happy news.' It was a sunshine day for all of us and with many more to follow as I made calls for the positive of those in that school.

"Kindness and caring were not exclusive to where I taught, but in my community as well. And it wasn't limited to people, well, not entirely. There was an elderly woman I drove to and from church as she had no means of transportation. Then, I began to take her to church luncheons and to the beauty parlor where I would treat her. When she passed away, I took the responsibility of arranging for her beloved cat to be adopted by a kind person. As far as I know, the cat is still living with this family. That would make my friend happy and certainly does me as well.

"Overall, when I think about acting on good character traits that are mentioned in this book, I think: We need to be a positive role-model and remember that good character is not to be advertised by word-of-mouth, but is to be demonstrated by one's actions." (Hayes 2017)

5. "This story is about my friend Carlos' dog, Donnie, who was one of the happiest dogs on Earth. We used to joke around and say that, because of the way Donnie greeted his 'human buddy,' Carlos, when he came home from school. This was Donnie's favorite time of day. Donnie would wait somewhat impatiently by that door, anticipating its opening up so he could jump all over Carlos and show his excitement at seeing him. Donnie would bark, and try to lick Carlos's face. Carlos loved that. After having a snack, they would play with Donnie's favorite toy, eat, and hang-out together.

"These two were the best of friends. But, one day this wasn't the case as when Carlos came home from school expecting his dog to attack him with love, Donnie just lay on the floor looking sad. Carlos wondered, 'What could be wrong?' While sitting there he thought, 'I don't see Donnie's favorite toy. I wonder where that is?' Maybe that would cheer him up, or maybe I'll have to take him to the vet's.

"Carlos started to clean under the couches, and that's when he found Donnie's favorite toy. It was a ball inside another ball, which they would use to play catch until they got tired. The bigger ball had broken, and the smaller ball fell out of it. Carlos figured this might be what was making his dog so sad and unresponsive.

"Carlos looked at his best friend and said, 'Wait a few minutes. I see what happened here. I'm going around the corner to the pet store to get you a new toy. When he got back home, Donnie was still acting unhappy but looked up to see Carlos "holding-out" in front of him the new ball, his favorite toy.

"It's like a light switch went on as Donnie sprang up to grab it. The two played together for at least an hour and that play time happened every day with Donnie's greeting Carlos with the usual excitement when he walked through the door. Carlos told me that he discovered, and subsequently, so did I, that being caring isn't limited exclusively to one thing or another, but for that which we love." (Umanzor 2017)

DEFINITION OF FAIR

The word "fair" means to demonstrate to oneself and others in thoughts and actions: active listening as opposed to just hearing words, realizing that fairness means each person's getting what they "need," but not everyone's getting the same thing or what he or she wants. A person who is fair treats others with an open mind, not making judgments, but rather listening to others while trying to understand what is being experienced.

In order to differentiate between wants and needs the following eight concepts are seen as human needs (Frost, M. 1973): Success, positive self-image, security, knowing things by using a multi-modality approach to learning, explore, belong, love and be loved, and dream.

Three Examples of Being Fair

1. "When you asked me about being fair, what came to mind was when I was the Chief Academic Officer at a college in middle-America. There was a faculty member who taught accounting and he was known to be, formerly, very active and involved in campus life. I'd witnessed this as I was, fifteen years earlier, his student. I'll name this person John. He was definitely tenured when I came to accept the administrative position, and he was up for post-tenure review. All-in-all, it was a good review, as he was an excellent professor. Still, over time, he'd come to be known as one who just came on-campus and taught his classes and was not involved in any campus-life.

   "Meeting with the faculty member I realized I could have reprimanded him or chastised him in some way about his not being involved, but then I'd be misrepresenting myself and the core-intention of being fair to faculty, regardless of my knowing them previously or not. Subsequently, I suggested John enter an 'Improvement Plan' where he'd take-on committee participation or community service endeavors. John took the suggestion to heart and redid curriculum and found things that were rewarding to the Business Division, as well as community-building around our campus.

   "I recall that, a year after I made the suggestion to John about his 'getting involved,' he came to me in my office and related what a good idea that was and how revitalized he felt. John retired about seven years ago, but stayed really active, from what I heard, as I moved on to my Presidency at Molloy College here in Rockville Centre." (Bogner 2017a)

2. "It was mid-August a very long time ago when I came to understand what fairness meant. Well actually, there was a ten-year time span between full initial and full-fledged comprehension. I was standing in the archway of the entrance to our living room in upstate New York State. I was watching my older-by-ten-years sister and dad standing by the brown velvet chair. My dad took out and opened his wallet. He gave my sister three hundred dollars. She gave him a kiss on the cheek as she said 'Thank you', and left the room smiling.

"I seized the moment and walked forward and asked my dad for three hundred dollars. My dad questioned why I'd need that money. I explained that I was going to buy Gummy Bears, chocolate bars, and a few hot-fudge sundaes. He laughed and asked why I would expect him to give me money for such—how about this—frivolity. I doubt I knew the meaning of that last word, but continued with how he'd just given my sister that amount and it was only 'fair' he did the same for me. My dad explained that my sister needed the money to get some clothes for college, which she'd be starting in a few weeks.

"I recall very clearly as I reflect on that time, that my dad then said that being 'fair' didn't mean my getting the same amount of money as my sister. Fair was getting what I needed, and I did not need three-hundred dollars for clothes for college, as I was eight, and certainly no money for chocolate. 'What you have is a want and not a need'. 'Hmm,' I thought, 'that kind of makes sense,' but dad had stated his case, and while I wanted some money, clearly I knew, I would get none for chocolate or snacks. I walked out of the living-room rather dejected.

"Fast forward ten years. I'm now 18 and ready to go to college. The same brown velvet chair is in the living-room and my dad is getting out of it when I approach him and ask for three thousand dollars. He exclaims, 'For what would you need three thousand dollars?' I explained that I needed the money for clothes for college, and because of inflation the amount was no long three-hundred like he'd given my sister ten years ago, but now had increased a thousand percent.

"My dad said flat-out there was no chance of my getting that amount of money for clothes for college. I asked for two thousand and he replied in the negative again. Then, I tried with a plea for a thousand, and again I was met with an emphatic, 'No.' I exclaimed that this wasn't *fair*, and my dad explained that getting what I wanted wasn't an example of *fair*, while getting what I needed was an example. I said, 'Okay, how much do you think is a fair amount to give me for clothes for college?' He replied, 'Maybe five hundred dollars.' I replied with, 'Done! Great! That is fair!' My lesson was learned about the meaning of *fair* as receiving what one needed, but not the same thing as another and not what someone wanted. There had to be a need.

"In this story the author focuses on a desire for material things; money for candy. However, character traits are behaviors that more often than not address emotional needs or desires. For example, there's the desire or need to be cared for and/or about, as easily as there's need for attention to being able to rely on others because of their being trustworthy, fair, responsible, kind, respectful, and a good citizen. But still, it's important to emphasize that these traits, in order to give them to another, must first be owned by oneself." (After 1958)

3. "My husband and I both come from very close families, and have learned in the few short years we've been married that marriage is a give and take arrangement. When I say that I, by no means, refer to keeping score. I mean that my husband and I always do the right thing when it comes to spending time with our respective families. We both value the relationships we have with our parents, our siblings, and our extended family-relatives. We work hard to ensure that time with each group or individual is prioritized and that we are fair to each with our time we share.

"When my husband first came home from the Marines, we spent a great deal of time with his family over mine, and I was happy to do so because I knew just how deeply they missed him while he was away. When my father passed away a couple of months ago, my husband spent a great deal of time with my family over his, and he was happy to do so. For this I was ever grateful. We do fair!" (Panzarino 2015b)

4. "This story takes place when we were in our 40s. Roya came to work for me, and I could see from the start that she liked to learn. Our friendship-in-business grew and I asked her if she'd like to make an investment in the jewelry business I was thinking about starting. I explained we'd decide on who'd get what of the profits, and after some thought, I figured we'd split what we made 50/50, because that'd be fair. After-all, she was investing in this not-sure-it-will-work venture. There was definite risk-taking, but fair would mean we'd each get what we needed.

"Fair turned to responsible, as I was having heart problems and needed a new one. I was wearing an Elvad Left Ventricular assisting device for over a year. Roya took on many of the responsibilities of running the business. Then, I became A-1 on the list of heart transplant recipients and had a transfer on December 1st of last year. For that month of recuperation, Roya took over running our business. She could not have been more fair and responsible." (Majed Hanna 2017)

DEFINITION OF RESPONSIBLE

The word "responsible" means demonstrating to oneself and others, in thoughts and actions the following: pursuit of excellence, accountability, self-control, thinking before speaking, and reliability.

As Mara Moore (2017), an emergency room nurse explains, "I'm responsible when I'm on-time for where I am supposed to be. It also is demonstrated by the things I do for our children, like picking them up from school. Mara continues with, "There's getting to work for the night shift and staying alert. Then, there's being responsible at work by not being distracted, but being present and 'in-the-moment.' Also, my responsibility to my patients includes being compassionate and caring. Most people, I think, associate nurses with being caring and kind people, and it's part of the responsibility of the position, but still there's an inner drive to be that not just at work but outside it as well. These character traits are part of our personality as much as having a glass of water quenching a person's thirst."

Two Examples of Being Responsible

1. "For me, as a college professor, being responsible means writing the syllabus and then conducting a class in accordance with the rules of the institution. It also means showing compassion and being able to differentiate between students' needs and desires, their responsibilities impacting on the work they do for class."

   "Before that, it was my being accountable as vice principal and being the go-to person for teachers, children, and staff at our school. And, back in the early years of my education career as a teacher, being responsible meant modeling being a person of good character, as well as addressing students' emotional and academic needs and the curriculum at the grade level I was teaching."

   "As a daughter to an aging mom, I was continually responsible by acting as an interpreter in every aspect of her life. This was with regard to translating her words from Italian into English at doctors' offices or wherever I drove her, as she couldn't drive. My life was divided with responsibilities to my nuclear family and my extended family as well. I was there for my mother, and she was there for me. In turn, I set an example for my own children about being responsible in a caring and compassionate manner. My mom passed at ninety-eight years of age, and I only have thoughts of how wonderful she was, as the person I became is the one she modeled for me through her words and actions." (Sullivan 2013)

2. "I'm titling this sharing, Living by Example. The example setter was my oldest daughter, Jenn. She was sixteen at the time and the year was 2001.

That year Jenn announced that she wanted to work at a camp that summer. I told her that I was very pleased. Every father wants to see his children get to the point where they can start working and earn some money for themselves. She said, 'No dad, I won't be making any money. I'll be working as a volunteer for no salary'. I didn't understand why she'd do that.

"She explained that the camp is called Camp ANCHOR, and it's a camp for children and adults with special needs. 'I'm not even sure that I'll even get accepted. They have hundreds of kids applying, and they accept only about a hundred.' I didn't understand why she'd do that.

"She went on to explain that the camp lasted six weeks and wouldn't end until the second week of August. She had to commit to all six weeks because, if she didn't, she wouldn't get hired. She also knew that, every second and third week of August, our family spent our vacation at my parent's summer house in Myrtle Beach. Our plans couldn't change because she'd have a volunteer job at this camp, because we had to be back for school by the last week of August. She said that she was willing to forego going on vacation and to stay home with my parents if she got the job. I didn't understand why she'd do that.

"Well, she got the job and she committed herself, my very responsible daughter, and worked with adult campers who had special needs. When the camp started, she came back each day exhausted, but exhilarated. Every night at the dinner table she told us stories of all the great things that happened.

"All I remember is what she'd done, how great the campers were, and what a wonderful time she was having. I recall hearing how someone had peed in the pool again or how a camper had bit her by mistake, or how she had finally conquered the challenge of holding a camper over the toilet bowl with one hand while wiping the camper's behind with her other toilet-paper-covered one. I didn't understand why she'd do that.

"The summer went on, and Jenn's enthusiasm for the camp and the campers never waned. If anything, it got stronger. She told my wife and me that, towards the end of camp, there would be a show that the camp put on and each group of campers, including hers, would be performing. She asked, 'Could we go to watch?' It was on a Friday, and I would have to take off from work. I didn't understand, but I took the day off from work.

"The day of the show, it was in the mid-90's and humid. The ANCHOR parking lot was packed and we had to park on the grass. I couldn't believe that there were this many people there. I couldn't wait to get out of the sun and into the air-conditioned building. Maybe my oldest daughter had mentioned it at the dinner table, and maybe I wasn't listening, or maybe she didn't think it important enough to mention, but not only was there no air-conditioning, but there was no building!

"Everyone, the campers, the staff, the volunteers, all were in tents. These were hot and sweaty places. They were places/tents where you thought 'I can't-breathe this-hot-humid-air.' Once again it crossed my mind that Jenn had "given up" her vacation to work her summer in a tent with no pay?' I didn't understand why she'd do that.

"We found the tent that belonged to Jenn's group and she introduced us to her campers before the show. We met Mary, 45, and a mother of two who had been in a car accident years ago that left her with severe brain trauma and confined to a wheelchair. Mary managed a crooked smile and a broken hell-oh/hello. Jenn said that Mary had her good and bad days. Today was a good day. I couldn't help but think that Mary was about the same age as my wife and how it could have been my wife in that wheelchair.

"I was still thinking about Mary, so I was only half listening as Jenn introduced us to Billy, who was born with cerebral palsy and was also in a wheelchair. Then there was Liz, who had Downs Syndrome and was non-verbal. Next we were introduced to Tom. At 17, he was just a little older than Jenn, and he was autistic. He announced to me that he was Tom Reilly and that he was going to marry Jenn and that Jenn would be Mrs. Reilly. That snapped me out of thinking about Mary, and I wasn't really sure what he had said. I didn't have to worry about remembering what Tom had said because he repeated the same wedding announcement over and over and over again.

"Jenn introduced each one of her campers as she would introduce any one of her friends, because they were her friends. She treated each camper with respect, caring, compassion, patience, kindness, and an understanding and sense-of-responsibility that, I thought, was well beyond her years. She was doing things on a daily basis that I could never dream of doing. When we left, Tom came over and gave me the biggest, longest, and best hug that I had ever had in my life. I understood why he did that, and in that moment there was clarity about why our daughter had chosen to work at Camp ANCHOR. This was her calling!

"The aftermath of this story is that Jenn's enthusiasm rubbed off on my two other daughters, and they joined camp ANCHOR as soon as they were old enough to do that. Those two daughters stayed at the camp until they graduated from college. Jenn went on to become a teacher and still works every summer at the camp. She met a boy named Kevin a few years ago, whose last name happens to be Reilly. Jenn is now Mrs. Reilly." (Cino 2017)

JOURNAL AND/OR DISCUSSION QUESTIONS

1. What was your reaction to someone being a "caring," person and why do you think you have that reaction?
2. What was the definition for being "fair?"
3. What was your reaction to the two scenarios regarding being "fair" and why do you suppose you thought that?
4. What does "responsible" look like to you?
5. What were some thoughts, ideas, opinions, and/or feelings regarding the two anecdotes for being 'responsible'?

Chapter 7

Good Citizen: Trustworthy

CHAPTER OVERVIEW

As stated in the beginning of chapter 5, each trait addressed in the specified chapter is titled with the traits, then in the chapter there are character behavior definitions followed by anecdotes about where this trait was witnessed. Or, there may be a story having the time when the person involved, personally, acted on this trait. Such is the case for this chapter with the two culminating internationally recognized person-of-good-character traits of being a *good citizen*, and being *trustworthy*. The contributors are all speaking reflectively about a time in their lives that was of such emotional significance that it is remembered from a few years to decades later. Each definition is followed by one or two examples presented anecdotally. The chapter ends with "Journal and/or Discussion Questions.

DEFINITION OF A GOOD CITIZEN

People who exhibit the trait of good citizenship are those who play by the rules. "A good citizen respects the rights of others and supports governing agencies" (Byrne 2017). These persons support being a good sport by taking on a reasonable amount of responsibility while demonstrating regard for authority. Good citizenship means persons staying informed about the world around them, voting when asked to do that, protecting their neighborhoods and community, "helping those in need through volunteerism" (Bogner 2017b), protecting the environment and conserving our natural resources.

Then, there's encouraging others to take an interest through community ser-vice, walk the talk.

Three Examples of Good Citizenship

1. "It felt like something out of a Tennessee Williams play; something to the tune of 'I've always depended on the kindness of strangers.' You wouldn't think making a spontaneous trip to Barnes & Noble in New York City, where I live, would result in three hours in an Emergency Room, and two years of friendship.

   "It was a cold winter day. There was salt all over the street, but not in front of the Barnes & Noble. As I entered the door, an elderly man walked out and he slipped. He banged his head on the concrete and was immediately bruised with blood staining his forehead. He also had quite a gash in his finger. A small crowd gathered, specifically an employee of Barnes & Noble who was quickly obtaining demographic information and particulars of the incident. In this litigious society, it was no doubt that this was a protective measure. The man appeared disoriented but compliant.

   "At first, I was a bystander, a gawker if you must. Someone in the crowd asked if he wanted to go to the hospital. He deferred, but seemed unable to assess his own need. He gave the impression of being more scared by the blood and the jarring of the accident rather than in any true pain. However, his forefinger was bent and hanging, appearing as though it had lost connection to the joint. The decision seemed to have been made for him, as the ambulance arrived.

   "At that point, I felt witness to a feeble, shaken old man who, though surrounded by a group of caring citizens, appeared fearful and alone. Of course, I had somewhere to be and a million things to do. *What should I do?* What does it mean to be a good citizen? My reflective process didn't last long as I found myself asking him if he wanted me to accompany him. He simply nodded. I got in the back of the ambulance and escorted him to the hospital.

   "We began to learn about each other. He asked what I did for a living, where I lived, and about my family. He told me that he had a son who worked in trading, and he didn't want to call him, didn't want to bother him. His wife was deceased. As we rode to the hospital, he repeatedly expressed his gratitude, and I knew I had done the right thing. Of course, his appreciation validated my decision. But more so, it was the bond we established during that drive and during the three-hour wait in the hospital's Emergency Room. Two strangers in this vast city who came together, serendipitously, were truly curious about each other's lives and exchanged humor like old friends.

"If you think this was an act of kindness towards him, it's much deeper than that. It was an act of kindness that also served me. I gained so much from this experience: I empathized with his sense of feeling alone, of feeling like a burden—in that there was a kinship. I took a risk and had done what was for me being 'outside the box.' I embraced his vulnerability and, in doing so, connected to mine. I gave him me and that's all that was needed.

"Through this incident, I confirmed that in NYC you get what you give. You don't have to be anonymous, you don't have to be distant, and you don't have to be unfriendly. By allowing myself to give to him, I allowed myself to be given to. If that's not setting the stage for a true connection, I don't know what is." (Meyers 2014/'17c)

2. "It was a hot spring day in 2000, and I was driving home from teaching my college courses. I was on the road at rush hour with over an hour of driving yet to take place. I figured this was going to be one heck of a trip, because the air conditioner didn't work and it was just that kind of a day. Anyway, I heard this 'kathud' sound and figured the car to my right had something wrong with it, like a flat tire. So, I "sped up" to get away from the car and the sound increased its repetitions.

"I thought, 'No, this can't be. My car has the flat. Ugh, I better pull over into that turnoff on my right.' Quickly maneuvering the car I pulled over, stopped the car, and turned off the engine. I got out and looked around the car as I noticed the passenger side rear tire was so flat that the rim was touching the ground. I did the only logical thing. I sat down cross-legged and cried.

"What seemed like only a few minutes, by looking at my watch, had been nearly a half hour when I 'felt' a presence next to me. I looked to my right and saw a pair of grungy looking sneakers with grease stained white socks and above that curly white hair on two legs that were also covered in grease. My eyes moving upward for hopefully a better appearance, I noticed khaki shorts, a white tank top with white hair profusely coming from it. And then, there was this person's face. There were teeth missing in the smile I saw. The facial skin was filthy, which meant more grease stains. I looked a little past this man and saw his dirty brown van that had no windows. I thought, 'This is it. No one can see me from the road and I'm going to meet my end here, at this time in this moment.'

"How many times had I said to my students and others not to judge a book by its cover? Well, that is exactly what I was doing as this 60+ man stated the obvious, 'You have a flat tire.' Then, he asked, 'Do you know how to change it?' The truth was I didn't know how to do that, and I admitted it. The stranger said, 'Then, let me help you. You must have a spare in the trunk.'

"I thought, 'Oh, the trunk, it's like a giant pocketbook for me. It's filled with students' Tri-fold Boards and school stuff. Neither he nor I will ever find the spare tire.' At this point, I used my cell phone to call my husband, and he spoke to the man, explaining it was a foreign car and the pouch was in the trunk along with the donut tire . . . somewhere under my things.

"To make a long story short, Harry backed away from the trunk when he opened it and saw it was loaded with 'stuff'!' But, he persisted and helped me unload the trunk, find the tire and tools needed to change it, and a few minutes later smiled the broadest smile of accomplishment when he'd changed the tire.

"I just looked at him and thanked all the powers that be for his assistance. Then, I asked him what made him stop, and he said he was just being a good citizen and helping someone in distress. Although I offered it, he'd accept no money for his act of kindness. He shook my hand, told me to have a nice day, and went on his way.

"Good citizenship is what was exhibited, and looking back I say I was lucky that Harry was who he was, a community-minded person who volunteered his assistance when needed. How much I'd taken for granted by his appearance and how much I was willing to label this individual with negatives. The end result is I learned that he was thoughtful, caring, concerned, trustworthy, and responsible, as well as being a good citizen. I hoped if someone needed my assistance one day that I could help that person as this man helped me. I also learned how to change a tire if it went flat, and forthrightly appreciate acts of kindness." (M. S. Schiering 2000–present)

3. "One time I believe I acted as a good citizen was in my senior year of high school when our school's music department went on a trip to Hershey Park. A couple of hours before we were leaving the park, my friend and I were walking to the bathroom and saw a little boy, who must have been no older than six years of age. He was walking alone, hysterically crying. At first, I thought that his parents might have been walking in front of or behind him, but I quickly realized that he had separated from his family and was now lost. Right before I went up to him to ask him if he was okay, he ran out the exit of the park, thankfully being seen by one of the Park's employees.

"Since you can't re-enter the park after you exit, I asked the employee if my friend and I could go run after him before he reached the parking lot, and she allowed us to do so. We ran out the exit up towards the parking lot and found the little boy wandering near the sidewalk, still hysterically crying. I approached him and asked 'Are you okay, Buddy?" All he did was start to cry harder. I then decided to pick him up and carry him back into the park, where I could bring him to security. He automatically clung to me, and I was glad that I was able to somehow comfort him when he was upset.

"By the time we reached the gates that the three of us had run out of, the employee we talked to before had already called security. While we waited for security to come, the little boy was able to calm himself a bit, but he still wasn't ready for me to put him down. After about ten minutes, a security guard arrived and took the little boy to search for his parents. Although I never found out if the boy found his parents that day, I am glad that I was able to notice the little boy and catch him before he wandered out of the parking lot and probably made his situation worse." (Miller 2015/2017)

DEFINITION OF TRUSTWORTHY

Being trustworthy involves honesty, integrity, promise keeping, and loyalty. In a more finite definition, sequentially: (1) honesty incorporates being sincere and loyal; (2) integrity involves standing up for your beliefs about the right or wrong of something. There's also resisting negative peer pressure and showing commitment, courage, and self-discipline; (3) Promise keeping is part of being trustworthy and it means keeping your word by not sharing a confidence with others that has been shared with you.

Don't divulge a confidence unless someone has threatened to harm themselves or others, and/or you are aware of emotional or physical abuse. Let students know that those are times when you do not keep a secret and neither should any one of them do that. Honoring one's commitments is a part of being trustworthy; *(4) Loyalty involves supporting and protecting family, friends, community, and country.*

Two Examples of Trustworthy

1. "As a hobby I collect anecdotes of some of the wonderful civic-mindedness of people in Maine. From my perspective this anecdote includes being kind, fair, caring, respectful, responsible, and having good citizenship. This particular story strikes me as almost from another era, and yet, here it is in the 2000s experienced firsthand.

"I was at the checkout in a supermarket over the summer of 2015, putting my groceries onto the conveyor belt. I was a little annoyed at the fellow behind me.

"He was putting his items onto the conveyor belt, and he was just assuming there would be enough room for his groceries and mine.

I thought, 'What was he doing infringing on my conveyor-belt space? Didn't he have the courtesy to wait his turn?'

"Anyway, it was a little before a friend's birthday, and as per her request, I was buying a prepaid Visa card for her along with the groceries. A little while after I left the store, maybe five minutes at most, I was about 20-feet into the dark parking lot. I heard someone shout 'Hey!' I turned around. The fellow who had been behind me had left his groceries to give me the Visa card I had left on the counter—the equivalent of $200 cash. There he was, this person I'd been silently complaining about infringing on my space, being respectful, kind, caring, fair, responsible, and displaying good citizenship all at the same time as being trustworthy. This was amazing and a wake-up call for me about what it is to be a person of good character!" (Borkum 2017)

2. "This is a story of compassion, kindness, trust, loyalty, and simply promise keeping between a student and his teacher. Julian was a student in my special education class. He had some behavior and academic challenges; however, he loved coming to school.

"We had a very special guest who brought all of the materials needed to plant baby spider plants in cups. The children in the class each got a cup to decorate. Then, they filled the cups with soil and planted these plants. Julian was so excited to be doing this with the class. After several days, the class was instructed to take their spider plants home with them. Julian got especially quiet. You could see he was thinking and that something was bothering him.

"At the end of the day, he came and said, 'Please Mrs. R. will you take my spider plant home with you and take care of it?' Of course, I asked him why, as he looked at me with sad eyes. He explained, 'I'm afraid the other boys will ruin it.' They don't understand this plant is really important to me, and I want it to be safe. I know you'll take good care of my plant, so I'm trusting you to do your best and put it on your windowsill and take care of it like it's your own.'

"I didn't even think for a second, as my response was, 'Of course!' Julian's relief was observable as a smile came across his face. He then asked me to make sure that, when his spider plant made sprouts, I would pass those sprouts along to other people. I agreed wholeheartedly.

"After many years that spider plant sits on my kitchen windowsill spreading shoots of baby spider plants. To this day, I've seen to it that friends and colleagues are recipients of one or more of those sprouts. When I pass along Julian's/my spider sprouts, I ask each recipient to do as I did and give a sprout away, paying it forward. I'm not sure how far and wide the spider plant has traveled, but I'm almost certain that love, caring, compassion, trust, being responsible, and kindness are passed along too.

"At a very young age, Julian recognized the qualities of a person of good character. This promise I made to him was easy to keep. And, I have taken every opportunity to share the plant, as I have this story. May you pass it along as well." (Rouse 2007/2017)

It's Almost Your Turn: Six Character Traits

Chapters 4, 5, and 6 have addressed the six international traits of being a person of good character. The definitions of respect, caring, fair, responsible, good citizen, and trustworthy were provided along with examples of each behavior. Following the questions for this chapter, the next chapter is for you to form groups and provide examples of these traits from your personal experience. This conversation starter and developer provides you with the opportunity either to lead or to partake in an activity designed to build classroom/whole-group community. And, from experience the author has had in using this activity for seventeen years, the participants come to realize the person of good character who is right next to him or her.

JOURNAL AND/OR DISCUSSION QUESTIONS

1. What were character traits and accompanying definitions of the three behaviors for this chapter?
2. Of the character trait stories, what were the ones with which you most identified? What do you suppose is the reason for this identification?
3. What were your thoughts on the principal's calling home with positive comments about the child? How do you suppose this action builds school and community?
4. Do you think that being "trustworthy" addresses all the person-of-good-character traits? Why or why not? And, if not, what trait do you think encompasses each one and why?

Chapter 8

It's Your Turn: Six International Traits of a Person of Good Character

CHAPTER OVERVIEW

This chapter addresses being a person of good character from your perspective. It's really an activity, as opposed to being one where there's information given with examples and/or accompanying activities, as in chapters 1–7.

Activity Purpose

The reason for this activity is to engage the participants in reflecting on what it is to be a person of good character and review the material in chapters 5–7. These chapters have set the examples for this one, as they have anecdotes explaining each of the six international traits of a person of good character. You remember these; they're trustworthy, fair, caring, responsible, respectful, and good citizen. When one is doing this chapter's activity, it is hoped that that person, regardless of age or grade level, will have ideas about each trait and a time when he or she either witnessed the trait or exemplified it, personally. Subsequently, there are identification and application of these character traits regarding how they have been experienced or modeled.

Chapters 1–4 have been leading you, the book's readers, to comprehend what it means to teach character development through a character education program. While there might be other programs available, this character development guide leads one to embrace self-awareness, the attributes of others, and, ultimately, *self-acceptance* by conversing *with* others. This activity in chapter 8 is about noticing the good in you. For a classroom of students, it's about that as well as recognizing the positives of those in that space, that shared environment.

This activity is one that can and is recommended to be done twice a month, if one is in a classroom setting. If not in a classroom, then you'd still want to do it on a regular basis. The thinking behind this idea is that there is a focus on positivity, and more exposure to that fosters such thinking in the school and elsewhere. This author relates that whenever you have the opportunity for thinking on the *plus side*, then take advantage of it.

CLASSROOM, HOME, OR CHARACTER EDUCATION WORKSHOP ACTIVITY: A PERSON OF GOOD CHARACTER

Respectful	Caring	Fair
Responsible	Good Citizen	Trustworthy

Figure 8.1. **Persons of Good Character**

Activity Directions

Separate, if possible, into groups of six. If there aren't enough people then at least have groups of four. If you're alone and want to do this activity, then be sure to have someone or a few others to share with at a later time and date. The chart provided in figure 8.1 has six boxes with a character trait in each one. The group members are to select one trait that was either personally exhibited or seen exhibited so the latter serves as a witness to the exhibition of the trait. Then, there is writing of that time in the box provided or on additional paper if needed. Be sure to let your group members know what trait was selected so repetition isn't in play.

After writing the anecdote like those presented in chapters 5–7, share the story with groupmates. If you've time to piggyback on a trait, then do that. In the classroom setting, this activity can take up to thirty minutes for this group-sharing portion of it. After everyone has shared, bring the class together, and select from each group one each of the traits for sharing. Again, do this activity once every few weeks. As the students get to know one another through their being a positive person who acts in a caring, kind way, the assemblage comes to know the "you" of you and the "self" of self. This is a bonding activity for classroom community and unity through recognition or practice of positive behaviors.

JOURNAL AND/OR DISCUSSION QUESTIONS

1. How would you evaluate your sharing?
2. What was your overall reaction to this activity?
3. Why do you suppose you had that reaction?
4. What did you learn from this activity about your classmates?
5. Did you find you could share on any of these character traits, and, if so, what ones? If not, why do you suppose that is true for you?

Section III

Chapter 9

Stressors That Impact Behaviors: When You're Not Being the Best "You"

CHAPTER OVERVIEW

In our daily life, we have situations that stop us from being persons of good character. That's simply a fact. While one would like to be kind, fair, trustworthy, and so forth, there are things that sometimes happen to stop this. This chapter provides a list of things that infringe on one's being a person of good character and the inner feeling with which it's associated. There's a group *activity* addressing five, author's impressions, of the greatest stressors, and what are the causes of stress. Then, a list of "possible stress relievers," compiled by this author, is provided. Michael Russo, PhD, has a few final thoughts he contributed in the "Mindfulness for Diminished Stress" section. The chapter culminates with "Journal and/or Discussion Questions."

DEFINITION OF STRESS

When the word "stress" appears, you probably tense and think of what stress feels like, physically and/or simultaneously, emotionally. Synonyms for stress include a sense of pressure and strain, anxiety, constant worry, discomfort, and/or nervous tension.

Two Stressful Times

One: What comes to this author's mind concerns a time she felt stressed more than fifteen years ago when her husband took over the cooking in their home. He willingly did this because he and every one of the six children complained about her cooking not being good.

The kids were off doing whatever at their after-school programs, and her husband was making dinner. As it turned out, he needed six ingredients to complete the meal. He needed these in a hurry. They live five minutes from the grocery store, and so he gave his wife the list of the items and sent her on her way. She figured, five minutes to the store, five minutes to get the items, five minutes to check out, and five minutes to get home. She said, "I'll be back in 20 minutes; will that work?" He responded in the affirmative.

The first two parts of the schedule were well executed. She got to the store and picked up the groceries in ten to fifteen minutes. Then, she went into the ten-items-or-less checkout line only to discover that the person in front of her had . . . are you ready . . . twenty-two items. The woman with these items was talking away with the checkout person, and she was oblivious to this author being annoyed. Feeling the tension rise in her at this ignoring her disdain, she audibly began counting the items the woman was putting on the counter. "And that would be item eleven in a line that says, Ten items or less." The checkout woman and the twenty-two-item woman acted as if no one were there, and if there was someone, that person was invisible. Then, in what seemed like a lifetime, the two said, "Bye," and it was the author's turn to check out her groceries.

Very annoyed, she asked the clerk if she'd noticed that she was checking out groceries in the "ten items or less line." She explained that she did, but that was her cousin, Barb, whom she'd not seen in months and they were so glad to see one another and get a chance to talk. She apologized for the author's being "held-up/inconvenienced." Watching the clerk check through her groceries she felt guilty. She smiled and went about her business. However, she'd now been gone for over half an hour and still needed to get home. *Stressed* is how she felt!

When she got home, her husband's first words were, "What took you so long?" Guess who was the recipient of her stress?

Do we think about what stresses us or our students? There are all sorts of things now as much as in the past. But with so much emphasis on meeting the curriculum requirements how often is time taken to address those things that bother us? One incident I recall was when teaching fifth grade.

Two: I was at my desk correcting papers and I saw my student come in early from recess and sit down at her desk crying. Seeing her continue to cry, I went over to find out about the problem she was having? She responded with, "My grandfather died." I told her I didn't think she should be in school and that I'd call home for her to see if she could go there. She quickly asked me not to do this because her grandfather died two years ago. This was the anniversary of his passing, and she was still affected by it. We talked for a bit of time, as K taught me that an incident from one's past may well carry over to today, and be the cause of discomfort we know as stress.

DISCUSSION POINTS FROM CHARACTER DEVELOPMENT WORKSHOP

"Sharing with a partner or two, please first reflect on and then write down your THOUGHTS, IDEAS, OPINIONS, JUDGMENTS AND FEELINGS about causes of stress and *why* or *how* one is impacted by these stressors. Be sure to discuss and include how you think these relate to bullying, prejudice, harassment, and discrimination. You'll be asked to make a group list in a few minutes.

"Please note that stressors impact on belief and value systems, as well as social cognition and experiences. Subsequently, stressors, because they are outside the norm of what you or your group accepts as being 'okay,' serve as the primary cause of anti-social behaviors and/or those related to bullying, harassment, cyber-bullying, discrimination, or prejudice. Prejudice is often-times exhibited towards race, color, weight, national origin, ethnic group, religion, religious practice, disability, sexual orientation, age, or gender." (M.S. Schiering 2000–present)

CLASSROOM, HOME, OR CHARACTER EDUCATION WORKSHOP ACTIVITY: STRESSORS AND CAUSES?

Activity Purpose

The reason for this activity is, first, to discover universal stressors and then realize plausible causes of these. Knowing what causes stress may help those involved with it or bystanders to demonstrate, in their comprehension of it, caring and compassion. However, first one needs to be familiar with what brings about the feelings of discomfort. These feelings may include bullying, prejudice expressed toward an individual who's considered different from others, or harassment and/or discrimination. Nonetheless, after the "Activity Directions" section, there are over fifty common stressors listed in paragraph fashion. The list was compiled by M. S. Schiering between 2000 and the present time from conference attendees in the United States, Europe, and South America, as well as Norway. The list is followed by figure 9.1, which gives over ten causes of "stress," and the causes of those stressors. These are not in order of importance but given as being important stressors and originate from the aforementioned locations.

Activity Directions

This activity was designed by Schiering in 2000 and is explained as follows: What the class is to do is be in small groups and select what they think are *five of the greatest stressors*. Consensus needs to be reached on the selection of these five. The five are shared with the class, and these are placed on a two-column piece of chart paper or the room's chalk/white board. Please do this on the left side. Next, working as a class unit, the students are to think of reasons why these are stressors and these will be listed on the right side of the paper.

List of Stressors

Death of a family member, Divorce, Parent/family vacation, Fear of or loss of job or change in job status, Fear of abandonment, Moving to another geographic location, Making friends, Addition of another adult or sibling to the family, Supervisor or assistant change, Theft of personal possession, Parental and/or sibling relationships, Home arguments, Change in family financial condition, Fear of failure, dogs, Close friend sick or injured, Self-illness or injury, Change in financial situation, Unexpected pregnancy, Trouble with grandparents, Fear of storms, Concern about car, Home conditions, Need for more money, Regimentation at work or children responding to school poorly, Fear of teachers/supervisor, Bullying (for adults this is usually sarcasm expressed in the workplace), Being put down or not appreciated, Too many activities, No time to relax, Family or relative/friend's alcohol or other substance abuse, Going away from comfort

BIGGEST STRESSORS	POSSIBLE CAUSES OF STRESS and/or WHY WE HAVE STRESSORS
1. Parent death or passing of a family member or friend 2. Parent or personal divorce 3. Change of family financial conditions 4. Fear of failure 5. Bullying 6. Lack of friends 7. Personal illness or injury 8. Sense of isolation 9. Fear of teachers 10. Changing schools 11. Drug or alcohol abuse 12. Moving to another geographic location 13. Trouble in school/Tests 14. Arguments with parents	• Instability • Loss or low sense of insecurity • Change of routine • Fear of the unknown • Lack of acceptance • Feeling isolated • Low self-esteem • Expectations not met • Isolation • Wanting but not receiving acceptance • Lack of acknowledgment for accomplishments • Too many put-downs and not enough lift-ups

Figure 9.1. Stressors and Possible Causes

zone, Traveling with others, Not having accomplishments recognized, Change of jobs, No job, Theft of personal item, Sibling rejection or dispute, Inability to cope, . . . Something not listed, but you think is tremendously stressful.

Possible Stress Relievers

- Converse *with* others.
- Hold discussions and have a sharing time as part of your everyday routine.
- Be an active listener = paying attention when another person speaks.
- Avoid/omit sarcasm and negative statements.
- Be *nice* to yourself and others.
- Collaborate, share, and cooperate by preventing scapegoating or pitting one person against another.
- Help enforce or reinforce empathy (ask about how another person feels, and share your own feelings).
- Model being responsible, and allow colleagues to express thoughts in a responsible fashion.
- Avoid being two-faced.
- Be true to yourself and others.
- Reach out to others.
- Make guiding statements.
- Emphasize good sportsmanship.
- Create opportunities to work together.
- Model and promote kindness through appropriate language.
- *Lead by example.*
- Teach and model courtesy.
- Admit your mistakes and seek to correct them.
- Give sufficient feedback when evaluating.
- Talk about the need to care for all living things, and regularly weave "What's the right thing to do?" into discussions.
- Practice mindfulness.

STRESS FACTORS WITH POSSIBLE SOLUTIONS

Self-Talk Thoughts for Relieving Stress

The booklet *Stress Therapy* (McGrath 1997) provides thirty-eight statements to say to oneself when addressing the topic of stress. The following five have been selected for inclusion in this chapter:

- "# 1 The best resource for managing stress is a fundamental faith that, beneath the apparent chaos, all is right with the world. Nurture such belief;

it's a foundation on which you can build a stress-management strategy that will improve your life."

- "#9 When you're feeling stress, you're more vulnerable to negative self-talk, that chronic criticism echoing in your head and heart. Counter the negative voice with affirmations about your ability and self-worth. Say, 'I'm talented, worthy, and loved,' and believe it."
- "# 10 Constantly trying to please others guarantees stress. You can respect and love others without living your life for them."
- "#12 Take a deep breath. Become mindful of your breathing. Draw your breath slowly from deep within your abdomen. Then, slowly exhale, releasing your tension and worry."
- "#17 Develop an attitude of gratitude. Making a list of blessings will put your worries in perspective. It's hard to be stressful when your heart is brimming with thanks."

Stress Activity Overview and Mindfulness for Diminished Stress

Through an activity calling for meeting consensus on five huge stressors out of fifty that were listed, this last section related the resulting cause of those stressors. It was presented that using this 'exercise,' we become aware of many things that bring on stress and thwart one's being a person of good character. How is it possible to get back to being one who is of good character by practicing kindness, caring, being trustworthy, respect, good citizenship, and responsibility? Perhaps practicing mindfulness is one solution for resuming those **good** character traits.

Professor Michael Russo (2015) from Molloy College addresses the topic of one's being *mindful* when it comes to paying attention, as it's this action that allows for focus on a specific stimulus without being distracted. He says, "When one is fully attentive to the situations surrounding him/her and concentrates on use of memory as well as orientation, the ability to make a decision and problem-solve takes on a new meaning which is 'directed thinking.'"

Paying Attention

Russo (2015) explains that "when one pays attention, his/her reaction to things changes. An individual sees more deeply as the mind and brain work in conjunction to *analyze* a situation at hand that is, let's say, stressful. 'By paying attention, you literally become more awake, emerging from the usual ways in which we all tend to see things and do things mechanically, without full awareness. This experience leads directly to new ways of seeing and being in your life because the present moment, whenever it is recognized and honored, reveals a very special and magical power: it is the only time any of us ever has. It is the only time we have to perceive, to learn, to act, or to Change. Practicing mindfulness can alleviate stress."

"Mindfulness is one way of thwarting stress that causes discomfort and, therefore, has potential for diminishing stress or impressions of the situation causing it. Let's examine mindfulness concerning stress: Being mindful, calls for assessment of the tensions one has by sitting with him and focusing on him and exploring the problem to provide a solution that will be tried for that time tension builds."

Getting in Contact

Russo continues, "Providing students with the opportunity to get in contact with the content of their thoughts and emotions is a powerful experience indeed. The practice of mindfulness is applied to strong emotional-feeling states like anger, fear, or desire. Students learn to observe these emotional-feeling states as they reveal themselves, without adding mental content and without judging them as either good or bad, but impacting their reactions and expression of self. The practice of observing these feeling states and treating them with some degree of objective-detachment can be an extremely liberating experience. Imagine practicing mindfulness not just to thwart stress, but also to eliminate it from one's daily experience. It's doable."

JOURNAL AND/OR DISCUSSION QUESTIONS

1. Looking at the Discussion Points in this chapter, determine how that may have been helpful in diminishing stress. What could you add to that exercise? Explain your answer.
2. What are the stressors you think your family members or classroom students may have?
3. What are the stressors of friends? List them. And in a small group, come up with four ideas to help reduce stress in those situations.
4. How might mindfulness impact on stress in a positive way? Explain your answer.

Chapter 10

Eradicating Bullying

Joshua Schiering

CHAPTER OVERVIEW

Joshua Schiering is LINX LLC vice president, camp director, trainer, speaker, and lifelong advocate for building a bully-free environment. He relates that much of character education relies on (1) antibullying methods, as well as (2) antiharassment, (3) antiprejudice, and (4) antidiscrimination techniques. These last three social cognition situations are most often experienced through bullying.

The focus for this chapter is to read this author's ideas and then share the contents of the pages with your opinion expressed to others. This is a chapter designed to formulate a discussion and for practicing the bully prevention techniques. Addressed are topics determining who decides who's being bullied and whether eradicating bullying is possible, to name just two such things. Creating a "positive-rich" environment is given attention, along with a true story that exemplifies putting the ideas of this chapter into the character development program. "Journal and/or Discussion Questions close the chapter."

TWO NEGATIVES MAKE A POSITIVE, RIGHT? NOT WHEN IT COMES TO BULLYING!

A single negative comment or act can have a lifelong and irreversible impact on a person. Whether in camps, schools, families, playgrounds, and even playgroups, bullying is a natural part of cultures. But, it doesn't have to be that way anymore. As individuals, we are empowered to make decisions about our actions. How we react to what we see and hear is up to each person. When it comes to bullying, I always challenge my staff and children to be countercultural in their decision-making.

BULLYING DEFINITION

Bullying is represented by the use of superior strength, influence, force, threat, or coercion to abuse, intimidate, or dominate others aggressively. The behavior is often repeated and habitual while there is an imbalance of social or physical power. Bullying may consist of one or more of these four basic types of abuse: emotional, verbal, physical, and cyber. Synonyms for bullying include persecute, oppress, tyrannize, browbeat, harass, torment, intimidate, strong-arm, and dominate.

Is It Bullying?

Some say the term *bullying* is overused and doesn't apply to all cases of meanness. I say, "Listen to the victim!" So, who gets to decide if an action is bullying? The answer is clear and simple: The victim alone decides if he is being bullied. While a single act of calling someone a name may not appear to fit into the definition of bullying, I challenge us all to take a closer look. Did being called that name make the victim feel intimidated? Did the name-caller have an implied power differential over the victim? As a result of this action, did the victim have a hard time focusing on schoolwork? Was he or she afraid of a repeat of the action? Did anyone feel oppressed? When it comes to feelings, well, no one gets to tell someone else what's being felt. Therefore, the victim decides if he or she is being bullied. Period! End of discussion!

Take It Seriously!

As educators and role models, we must take every reported and observed act of meanness seriously. While as adults we may have thicker skin and our life experiences help us handle the intimidating actions of a bully, the issue a child is facing might be the most significant and biggest deal in that person's life. We must let children know that, as adults, we do the following: hear them, take what they are saying seriously, are there to help now and in the future, coach and train them, will make sure justice is served, will make them whole again, and will hold the aggressor/bully accountable for actions.

ERADICATING BULLYING—IS IT POSSIBLE?
I SAY, "YES!"

When we sit down with our children before the start of a new school year to discuss their goals in school, we do not say, "Let's try for C's across the board." We encourage and motivate them to strive for all A's. We acknowledge it will be tough, and it will require a lot of hard work, but nonetheless, we work for the best possible outcome. Subsequently, when it comes to bullying, I encourage all institutions to take a stand and declare their initiative to eradicate bullying. We are not in the business of 'dealing' with bullying, we are in the business of not allowing it to exist in our environment. So, how do we eradicate it?

eradicate (verb: i'radi͵kāt): destroy completely; put an end to. Synonyms: eliminate, get rid of, remove, obliterate.

To Eradicate Bullying, We Must Do Two Things

1. Train parents, staff, and children on how to handle bullying when it happens regarding:

   a. how to see it; and
   b. how to address and remove it immediately.

2. Create an environment so rich in "positives," that bullying would never have a chance even to enter the environment by doing the following:

   a. Set goals and expectations that everyone be kind, respectful, and inclusive.
   b. Share your goals with others (colleagues, supervisors, etc.).
   c. Motivate effectively so those involved want to exceed your expectations.
   d. Get buy-in from your staff (have each person as a contributor at your goal-setting meeting so each feels a connection to the mission).
   e. Get buy-in from your children/students/campers and parents (have your staff facilitate the goal-setting meeting the same way you led the meeting with them).
   f. Never let your guard down, and never give up this mission.
   g. Celebrate your accomplishments (Celebrations at home can be extra story time, special outing with a parent, etc. Celebrations at school or camp can be a dance, carnival, game the children want to play, etc.)!

I am known for saying, "I would rather lose one mean camper from our actions, than lose a single camper because of the actions of one mean camper." These are strong words to stand by, but parents, staff, and campers know I mean business, and therefore no one in our environment will stand for acts of meanness. As a result, campers feel safe and encouraged to try new things without fear of rejection, humiliation, or put-downs. The result is a community in which people are free to fail, and therefore more likely to learn, due to the supportive environment provided everyone.

Follow Through

All too often, institutions have a great method for handling bullying, but they tend to forget one of the most critical steps of them all: *follow through*. If we fix a car that is leaking oil we can't assume it is fixed forever, and so we check the source of the leak as time goes by. We make sure there is nothing dripping from the area we fixed, and we make sure there are no new leaks. If there are more leaks, or the same area we fixed leaks again, we take it back to the shop to be fixed again.

A customer should leave the shop feeling that he or she has been encouraged to come back if there is another problem. It is much the same when working with children. They should feel welcomed and encouraged to return by having been provided with feedback that addresses present and future concerns and problems. Every issue must be dealt with, or all of our efforts leading into the "fixing/eradicating" of the problem are for naught. So follow through and follow up often.

Example: My plumber Jamie recently installed a garbage disposal at my house. When he left, he said, "Keep an eye on it, and look for leaks. If you see anything, let me know and I will come back immediately." Jamie is not only an excellent plumber (no leaks) but also he made sure I felt comfortable to come back to him in the event of a problem. Even if it is in a year, I will go to Jamie, because I know he cares and stands by his word/work.

Be like Jamie when it comes to working with kids who come to you!

Training

How to see bullying:

- Have appropriate staffing ratios. Give your team a chance to see and hear everything. Not just in the classroom but on the playing fields at recess, on the buses, and all around.
- Build relationships based on trust. Your team will not see and hear everything that happens, for they just can't. So building a relationship of trust

will make the victim more inclined to come to you in cases you don't see or hear what happened.

- Promise and follow through on anonymity. Children need to know they can trust you, and need to know they won't get in trouble for telling you something.
- Remember this—"Silence is approval." If you see bullying or it has been reported to you, you must act!

How to Address and Remove Bullying:

- Handle each situation with "kid gloves."
- Take what a child shares, seriously, and remember that, if you think it is a small deal, it is likely a big deal to the person reporting the incident to you.
- Remove the child who was victimized, and listen to the story with compassion and concern; let him or her know you are there to help him or her. And let him or her know you are proud he or she came to you! You want to encourage this action and therefore must provide positive reinforcement for this behavior.
- Remove the aggressor from the situation, and have a one-on-one
- Remember that perception is reality. While you might get conflicting stories, you need to listen carefully and find the right balance to help both parties come to terms and own their actions/decisions;
- Communicate with the home! Parents are there to help raise their child and need to be in the know.

Create an Environment Very Rich in the Positives

If you go to your doctor and you learn you have high cholesterol, you have a few options to help your situation. You can improve your diet, or you might take medicine or be more active. Each of these steps, like the bully-response plan discussed previously, is a reactionary one. What if you took the steps to ensure that you never had high cholesterol in the first place? What if you ate well and exercised your entire life? You are ahead of the game and might never know life with high cholesterol!

Remember that bullying is part of human nature and what we are trying to do is to be countercultural or create a different, more positive cultural habit and habitat. It will take time and patience, but you must succeed! Be a change agent.

Establish Expectations and Rules for Your Group

You must have a meeting within the first fifteen minutes of a group's coming together for the first time. Any time a new member enters the group, you must sit together and review the rules collectively. In this gathering, never dictate the rules; you want "buy-in" and "ownership"; you are a facilitator. You can, of course, lead the group to the answers you want by using leading questions (should we be respectful . . .? what should we do when . . .?).

The outcome of this conversation must include words with powerful meanings, explanations, and examples, like respect, kindness, inclusion, fairness, taking turns, cooperation, good listening, good sportsmanship, and spirit. Solidify this discussion by making a sign, poster, creed, or bill of rights. You decide. But, get everyone in your group to agree to honor this list of rules and expectations.

Then, hang it up, or carry it with you. If the occasion arises, you might need to reference the list and remind children what we *all* agreed to uphold. Next, put positive reinforcements in place. Many schools and camps use different models for this, and each is adaptable to a home situation too. Whether filling a jar with marbles for each time a rule is followed or expectation exceeded, or giving a high five, be sure to recognize and celebrate achievements!

Evaluate your plan. Do this on your own as the administrator, or do it with your group. Have debriefs and discussions to check how things are going. Publicly provide positive recognition for behaviors you asked for when you see them.

Story: Lesson

One day I went up to the softball field and saw two lines formed (partners throwing and catching across the field). The coach told the girls that for every successful catch they made, they got a point for their team. Girls were motivated not to fail at catching. Before they started throwing, I asked the girls to define good sportsmanship and explained that I wanted to see them being good sports during this activity. The second I heard one child say, "nice catch" to her teammate, I jumped all over it! I immediately said aloud, "Ooooh! . . . great, good sportsmanship encouraging your teammate!" What followed was inspiring, every single player shouted to their teammate words of encouragement: "Nice catch, ooh . . . good try . . . you'll get it next time, way to go!"

The lesson here is that kids are innate people pleasers. Tell them what you want, motivate them to exceed your expectations, and then acknowledge them for their efforts and accomplishments. In this softball catch game example, my praise was all it took to get them to do what I wanted. With younger children you might need to use point systems, sticker charts, games, and other strategies.

What you've been reading comes down to this: You do not tolerate negative behavior, and you maintain a zero tolerance policy for any acts of meanness. You do that and follow the plan we discussed earlier, and you will succeed. Is it true that if you demand perfection, you will get perfection!

I say, "Set the expectation for perfection, and then give the people the tools needed to succeed and motivate them properly to exceed your expectations and watch the magic."

Book Author's Reactionary Comment for Eradicating Bullying

When sharing Joshua's article in character development workshops and classrooms, I have discovered the strong positive reaction to the beginning statement about the person being bullied deciding he or she is having that experience. This is seen as fair and just! Overall, the reaction has been that the organization of the article allows for comprehension of the topic in a logical way. However, of greatest importance were the steps to be taken to eradicate bullying being outlined in a concise manner with the realization that each of us can change what is happening through an act of one's personal determination.

You could liken the message in these pages to the story about Beth, found under the "Being Respectful" section in chapter 5 of this book. That individual took action to stop bullying. Each of us may do the same. Doing so is a question of "acting" on such a decision. You are responsible for you. You can make a change happen that's directed toward antibullying, if you choose to do that. Perhaps the thing to do is to say to yourself this: "If I do nothing, then nothing will get done. I am responsible for eradicating bullying and the best time to do that is NOW"! (M. S. Schiering 2000)

JOURNAL AND/OR DISCUSSION QUESTIONS

1. What is your overall reaction to Joshua's ideas on eradicating bullying?
2. What were the most important messages you received when reading these pages?
3. What are some ways (list at least four) that you could institute a bully-free class or school?
4. With whom would you start having a bully-free environment?
5. For whom are you responsible, and how does this impact on bullying?

Chapter 11

How to Accept an Apology: Empowering Victims and Educating Aggressors

Joshua Schiering

CHAPTER OVERVIEW

This chapter by Joshua Schiering focuses on the idea of reading and internalizing his thoughts regarding apology acceptance. How an apology is given and received is addressed. You're asked to read this author's viewpoints and then share the contents of the pages with your opinion expressed to others.

After explaining the common responses to an apology and other suggestions for this act, the author provides a worksheet for *apology training*. The idea of writing a sample apology letter or note is given. Then, sharing of this in a classroom with students doing the same thing as a result of scenarios provided by the teacher is given. Sharing the apology letter with another is suggested for reactionary purposes. "Journal and/or Discussion Questions" close the chapter.

GENERAL APOLOGY REACTION

More than 95 percent of the time, the response to an apology is, "It's okay." Go ahead, test it out for yourself. Even as adults, we tell *aggressors*, "It's okay." Why do you suppose we do this?

Some answers are that it's quick and easy and we believe we can all move forward. But, here are a few questions to ask ourselves:

- What do we learn from the quick and easy way out?
- What do we teach others about how to treat us in the future?
- Was the act committed against us truly "okay," and if it wasn't, then why do we tell the *apologizer* that it was okay?

DEFINITION OF APOLOGY

Apology *(noun: a·pol·o·gy): an acknowledgment expressing regret or asking pardon for a fault or offense.*

Examples:

1. "We owe you an apology."
2. "My apologies for the delay."
3. "I make no apologies for supporting that policy."

Synonyms: expression of regret, confession, act of contrition, excuse, explanation, admission of guilt, result for forgiveness.

The quick, "It's okay" is counterproductive to our goal of *empowering the victim and educating the aggressor.* It sweeps the issues under the rug. It might toughen up our skin for the next time, but what we really learned is just to 'look out' for that person in the future. We learned not to trust *that* aggressor. We learned to hide our true feelings and not stand up for ourselves.

Children are often "told" or "forced" to apologize by adults who do not take the time to truly process what has transpired. People often need time to process what was done to them, what was said to them, and how it made them feel. Rushing into a quick apology and a quick acceptance of the apology is a *big* mistake.

I once had two campers, Johnny and Timmy. They got in an argument when Johnny ripped a Buzz Lightyear figurine out of Timmy's hand while saying, "Give it to me, dummy!" Well, I immediately swooped in and made Johnny give back the toy and *apologize at once!* Regrettably, moments later, the boys were at it again. Johnny learned nothing from the "forced" apology, and Timmy was not equipped with the tools to stand up for himself, as he wept in sorrow for being overpowered yet again.

Lesson Learned: We must take our time when it comes to *sincere* apology giving and receiving.

Definition of Being Sincere

sincere (adjective: sin cere): free from pretense or deceit; proceeding from genuine feelings.
Example: "They offer their sincere apology to Lisa and Johnny."
Synonyms: heartfelt, wholehearted, profound, deep.

Empowering the Victim

The Apology Training Worksheet (given in the following) teaches us how to *empower the victim while educating the aggressor.* The training is designed to establish the tone for the group and creates an environment of support, responsibility, and accountability for one's actions. Admittedly, it takes a lot more time than the conventional method of facilitating a quick apology, but in the long run, the benefits outweigh the investment of initial time by a factor of 100.

Accept These Comments as Facts

- Acts of meanness and bullying are to be treated as seriously as, and at times more seriously than, a physical act of aggression
- While children are capable of amazing things, they can also:
  - be mean;
  - hurt feelings;
  - cause each other to cry;
  - make someone not want to go to school or camp; or
  - make people feel like they just don't belong.

*Please note that adults are capable of these acts as well. As people, and most importantly, as educators, we are also capable of doing the complete opposite!

The Apology Training Worksheet

Listed in the following is a sample interaction between two children with a camp counselor assisting along the way (the counselor could easily be a parent, teacher, bus driver, lunch supervisor, etc.). This scenario can be applied to any situation, at any age.

Scenario

Johnny told Lisa that he didn't want to be friends with her because she was "gross." The facilitator observes the situation and has the two campers step away from the group. While kneeling down to the height of the campers to make eye contact and not to appear intimidating by looking down, he reviews what took place.

Facilitator: Johnny, do you have something to say to Lisa?

Johnny: I'm sorry.

Facilitator: Johnny, please look Lisa in the eyes when you apologize. Please try again and say why you're apologizing.

Johnny: I'm sorry for saying you are gross (this time making eye contact).

Facilitator: What do you say, Lisa? (knowing 99% of the time the child will respond with, "It's okay)

Lisa: It's okay.

Here is where the training applies.

Facilitator to Lisa: But, was it okay that he said that to you?

Lisa: No. (Be sure to get the recipient of the brief apology to say it was not okay.)

Facilitator to Lisa: If you forgive Johnny, let him know you forgive him, but let's also share why it wasn't okay.

Lisa: I forgive you, but it wasn't okay.

Facilitator to Lisa: Now, let's tell Johnny why his apology wasn't okay by explaining that you do not deserve that and it's not okay to be mean to you. Ask him not to repeat this behavior. Don't do that again.

Johnny (with assistance from Facilitator if necessary): I am sorry and I will not do it again. You are right. Lisa. You do not deserve to be spoken to that way.

Facilitator: I am very proud of both of you. Lisa, you did a great job sticking up for yourself. You never have to let people be mean to you. Johnny, though you were mean, you apologized and took responsibility for your actions. I know you heard Lisa and now know that you cannot treat her that way again. I don't want you to treat anyone like that. (Facilitator would ask Johnny how he would like it if he was treated that way.)

Now, let's work together, be nice to one another, and work to earn respect from everyone in our classes.

Immediate Results

- Empowered children who can trust adults and now have the support needed to stand up for themselves are ones who know justice has been served.
- An environment is created in which the *aggressor* knows that the institution and the adults and children involved will not tolerate this behavior.
- *Victims* and *aggressors* now have the words to use the next time this type of situation arises.

Long-Term Results

- More confident children who know how to stand up for themselves;
- Children who can trust their adult role models to be there for them;
- Children who respect others and themselves;
- Team players focused on working together toward a common goal (being kind to others and earning positive reinforcement established by the leader).

Follow Through

The last steps include circling back to the children later in the day and week to make sure everyone is being respectful and supporting one another. Parents of both children may be contacted, as necessary, to inform them of the situation, how it was handled, and how it progressed for each child. Parent conferences might be required as well depending on the severity of the situation.

Training at Camp

The following training techniques are provided for a camp setting. However, this can be changed to a school's classroom or workshop by number of attendees and use of the word *instructor* or *teacher*.

Ice Breaker Activity

Circle your team up (up to thirty at a time) and have a staff member sitting next to you who is holding a piece of paper (perhaps a paper you handed out). As everyone is settling into their seats, and the attention is now on you as the facilitator, harshly grab the paper from the person next to you, while saying aggressively, "Give me that!" You will get everyone's attention really quickly. Then, look to the person, and hand him back the paper and say, "I'm sorry, my bad." The person will surely reply, "It's okay." You can then launch into the training by asking him, "Was it okay? Was it really?" Enjoy the rest of the training by using volunteers to role-play this scenario.

Parent Training

It's easy for moms, dads, and caregivers to make use of this training. You do not need a formal sit down; just do it, and watch what happens! It takes all of about three minutes (typically). Be consistent, and do it the same way each time. Eventually, you will be able to ask leading questions, and they will start to do it on their own. Trust me, it works!

A Typical Teen in Action

I recently got a call from my son's teacher about his misbehavior in class. My son, age thirteen, was not excited when I called for a meeting between him and the teacher. We went into the school together, and his mood was, well, as you can guess, not enthusiastic. We sat down with his teacher and I quickly shifted into the role of facilitator.

I asked if she could explain for Jake what it was that he did wrong so he could hear it directly from her (previously he heard about his being disrespectful in class only through the e-mail I shared with him). Keep in mind that my son was dumbfounded by the charges and felt attacked and singled out, when surely there were others who had done worse (common reaction by teens). Of course, I explained to my son that I did not care about the actions of the others in his class and that he *must* own his decisions and be prepared to face the consequences and make it right.

After Jake's teacher explained his behavior and how it was counterproductive for the class objectives, he digested what was shared, and we slowly worked to get the apology out of him. Now I did not give his teacher a chance to say, "It's okay," as she was starting to mutter those words once he initially simply said, "I am sorry," but I had him continue. I prodded him (with words and a few nods of my head) and instructed him to answer: "Why was it not okay to do that? Will you do it again going forward? Why won't you do it again and what does your teacher deserve?" I then asked him if he was capable of doing what was right, and if he would commit to making good decisions of which he could be proud.

"Well," Jake cried (I think mostly because of embarrassment), but he got through it and the teacher said she appreciated the apology and his owning his actions. Jake's report card came out a month later, and his teacher's comment was that he had shown improvement in class (behaviorally). I recently sent an e-mail to the teacher (two months later) to see how he was doing, and she reported that his work and behavior were terrific. A little training can go a long way, and in this case, the fear of embarrassment and being held accountable for bad actions, I suspect, helped get my son back on the right path.

By the way, I have to share that when I got the e-mail about my son's being rude and disrespectful in class, I was appalled! I was even more appalled when he tried to deflect the behaviors and decisions he made to his friends. I thought, "My son did what?!!!" Then he played the "I didn't do anything" card. Well, that was when I knew I had to have a face-to-face meeting with the teacher. Had he owned up to it right away, he might of gotten away with simply writing a sincere apology card (a tool I use for campers as young as three years old).

Apology Cards

Apology cards are a great technique to use at home and school to get aggressors to reflect on their actions. Instead of the quick apology, remove the aggressor from the situation and have him take the time to reflect on what he did. Younger children can draw a picture and dictate the written apology to the adult, while older children (first grade and up) can write the apology themselves (pictures can also be included, and in some cases, an art project can also be made to help with tactile learners who need to use their hands).

After the "time-out/apology card" time is up, the aggressor delivers the note and apologize face-to-face. Doing this activity really makes the aggressor take the necessary time to reflect and consider the victim's feelings. It also enables the facilitator to assess the situation and determine if parental interaction is needed (if there is no remorse, I typically send the child home for the day and require an in-person meeting with parent and child the next morning).

CLASSROOM, HOME, OR CHARACTER EDUCATION WORKSHOP ACTIVITY: APOLOGY CARD SAMPLES AND MAKING AN APOLOGY CARD

Using one of the two scenarios provided, as well as observing the samples provided in Figures 11.1 and 11.2, make an "apology card" to be shared in the class (L. Schiering and M. Schiering 2014).

1. You're in the hallway and bump into a person causing his or her books to fall on the floor.
2. You went to a friend's house and, instead of sharing his computer you totally monopolized the time on it.

Figure 11.1. Landyn's Apology Card

Figure 11.2. Marina's Apology Card

Closing Comments

We are proud of the work we do on a daily basis. We believe wholeheartedly
that we are able to bring awareness of apology training to the world, one staff,
one parent, or one child at a time. Now, once you have this system in place,
the learning and growth of the individual and community are limitless! You

have to believe in this and set the course as the leader of your organization, classroom, or school for it to work. Inspiration and mission setting are important! Passion for a cause is inspiring. Go forth and inspire by being positive role models for children and others! Realize that how to accept apologies is also indicative of ways to give them.

Book Author's Closing Comments

Having used Joshua's *accepting an apology* techniques in a classroom and workshop, I have found them to be most beneficial for calling attention to what we take for granted. This is with respect to how we may accept an apology and how we may give it. One further thought is that when we do something that clearly requires an apology that we learn how to forgive ourselves for what was done to require it. While giving an apology for the purpose of being forgiven by another, we need, simultaneously, pardoning of ourselves with a determined will not to repeat the behavior or the ones like it.

JOURNAL AND/OR DISCUSSION QUESTIONS

1. What were two main points of this chapter?
2. What are ways you can teach others to apologize?
3. What is a good way to accept an apology?
4. What did your sample *apology card* emphasize for you?
5. How is one's ability to accept an apology like one's ability to give an apology?

Chapter 12

Character Education/Development: Making Decisions

CHAPTER OVERVIEW

This chapter explores the concept that decision-making is something which children and adults are faced with each day. However, one's skill at this task may be limited, because of lack of practice. Part of character education and character development involves making choices. A method for decision-making/problem-solving is presented in a graphic organizer format and then a narrative example. The chapter closes with "Journal and/or Discussion Questions."

HISTORY REGARDING DECISION-MAKING

In the social cognition model in chapter 3, there are sections referring to the cognitive collective, beliefs and values, and social experiences. Looking at the last of these, it's obvious that school classrooms, at any grade level, are involved in social experiences, as well as academic ones. The latter of these refers to a curriculum that is assigned to a particular grade level.

The curriculum must be met! How that curriculum is taught includes instructions on what is to be done, when this will occur, how the assignment is to be met with materials provided, and whom one will work. All this is at the ready. The day's schedule is often placed on the board for easy viewing. The one thing missing is the students' involvement in deciding anything. They are the followers of instructions, the doers in accordance with a plan set out for them well in advance of arriving at school. In the upper grades, some of those restrictions are eliminated and creativity may be part of some assignments.

Decision-Making: Preschool and Afterwards

Before school years commenced, there probably was some decision-making with reference to what to wear, such as formal or informal clothing, shoes or sandals, and so forth. Looking back on parental modeling, this author realized that for this generation and several before it, limiting choices of preschool children was to allow for yes or no, here or there, and/or this or that. Fundamentally, the choices were most frequently limited to two possibilities. Subsequently, a *pattern* was established, and that pattern stayed in place until school years came along.

In school, decision-making wasn't part of the objective as the daily schedule was placed on the board. If there were choices, then they'd be about after-school endeavors with what sports to play if any or something as simple as one's hairstyle. These, along with whether to go to a friend's house or a movie, and, if so, with whom, might have been on the agenda. For those decisions, most individuals had parents who gave permission before the answer was determined. Maybe there were more decision areas but not so with the number of choices, because the *pattern of two* was already ingrained in the mind-set of those decision-makers!

Social experiences call for decision-making and problem-solving. But if one hasn't had the experience on a regular basis or, when he did have it, these were limited to two possibilities, what happens is indecision. There are numerous issues in the social setting of a school where making up one's mind is necessary, and these are on a regular basis. One of the first ideas of this author regarding decision-making is, "With whom will the student be friends?"

Decision-Making Perspective

From an adult's perspective, decision-making might involve what's to be made for dinner, where shall we go on vacation, what car should we buy, or what cell phone is the best investment because of the features it has, and whether to go out on Saturday night. Those are all everyday occurrences. But, in the preceding paragraph, that student-in-school decision about friendship may result in many more decisions.

Then, let's say that sociocentricity kicks in and decisions are made within the group about places to go and things to try. Drugs might be one of those "should I try this" choices. Alcohol use and/or abuse and, although unpleasant to mention, suicide may be considered in extreme cases.

If one is not accustomed to making decisions, then he or she may let others decide for him or her, and one's own mindfulness is nothing more than doing what someone else says is "Okay." Advice in this realm may be good or not representative of being a person of good character. Certainly, doing harm to your body is not a good thing, but a decision often made from peer pressure and an inability to be discerning is rather commonplace.

The decision-making graphic organizer (DGMO) is presented to create a way to solve problems that involve an individual or small-group thinking about possible solutions to a stated situation.

For the DGMO, the problem is placed in a box at the top of the paper. Three choices are to be made and then three possible positive and three possible negative solutions to the stated problem are applied on the organizer. Then, reviewing what's on the organizer, one comes to a final decision with an explanation of why that choice was made.

The use of critical thinking is evident. Further analysis of the decision-making process is heightened when analyzing *why* a particular decision was formulated. Everyone benefits from seeing this process's scope and sequence by examining their own thinking and feelings, as they prepare to make decisions. Applied comprehension (understanding how the situation relates to you, personally) is evident with small-group activity involving collectively hearing one another's ideas and opinions to solve a presented problem.

PURPOSES OF DECISION-MAKING GRAPHIC ORGANIZER (DMGO)

"At the onset, the purpose of this graphic organizer is to have a realization of the steps taken for one to make a decision with the use of critical thinking— thinking that is reflective, important, serious, and in-depth. The process supports creative thinking as well when one comes up with the ideas for Choices and Possible Outcomes." (M. S. Schiering, 1976–present)

See figure 12.1 and examine the reciprocal thinking phases given in appendix A). Through discussion and instruction the one or several people doing the organizer realize (beginning awareness) that this either/or concept is replaced with the recognition of three options being most beneficial in problem-solving. It's at this juncture that it's apparent that not just critical and creative thinking are evidenced but concrete, structured thinking as well is in-play. The last of these is due to the format of the organizer.

Literature can be used to develop critical thinking and explore how decisions were made. Additionally, another purpose of decision-making is how it is incorporated into the process of a story with examining, through reflection, the rising action, climatic moment, and descending action leading to resolution. This is usually the climatic point of the narrative or expository writing.

Furthermore, collaboration and analysis may be provided through classroom discussion regarding the critical thinking used for the fill-in sections of a DMGO.

The ones doing this fill-in portion of the graphic organizer benefit from seeing and experiencing the process while examining their own thinking, as they prepare to make choices and examine the possible outcomes. In time, the decision-making process becomes natural, and the actual DMGO isn't needed. Cognitive awareness, critical and creative thinking, as well as the meta-cognitive processes become a key factor when constructing a DMGO, as it has been established as part of one's daily experience.

Teaching Decision-making

Making a decision can be taught, and figure 12.1 is one way to address this topic. You'll note that, in looking at the top of this graphic organizer, one sees a space for the "problem." This is the decision topic section. Then there are "three possible choices" that one thinks of for solutions to the problem. The reason for these three choices is to not limit an individual's thinking, but to be challenging at the onset. Having three choices calls for expanding one's thinking, and thinking is one of the major objectives of this activity.

Next, under each "choice" section, there is a section for "three possible positives" and "three possible negatives" that would be a potential result of that choice. The "final decision" section states the decision made and *why*. The material that is on the graphic organizer in the "possible outcomes" sections is what has to be mindfully addressed and stated as the reason for that decision. The student then is practicing mindfulness, discernment, and reasoning with comparing and contrasting the possibilities for "choices" and the aftermath of them.

DECISION-MAKING GRAPHIC ORGANIZER

Classroom Application of the DMGO

In the beginning, it is suggested that the class do a DMGO in small-group format or with the whole class. The teacher may use this opportunity to have guided practice and assist student learners with making the choices and filling in the possible outcomes sections. The main idea is to practice making decisions so, when one is alone or being influenced by others, the graphic organizer comes to mind and using in-depth thinking may lead to a solution to a problem that is viable, safe, and representative of a person with good character.

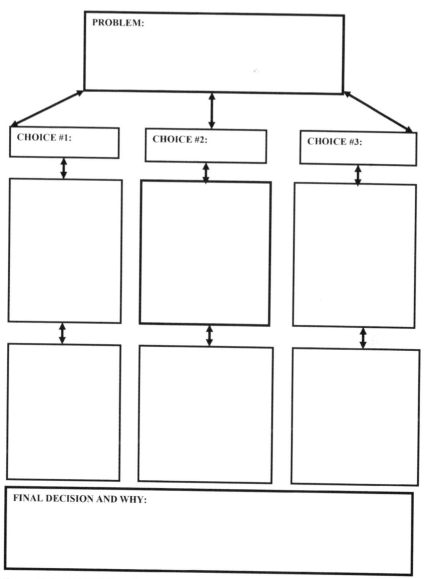

Figure 12.1.   DMGO Template

DMOG Example: Let's say the topic or problem is, as James Black (2017) exemplified in our interdisciplinary ELA and reading course: "What should I do if I win a million dollars? The "Choices" might be 1. Give the money to charity, 2. Give the money to my family to clear off anything they owe, or 3. Spend all the money on myself." (See figure 12.2 for James's DMGO on the topic of winning so much money.)

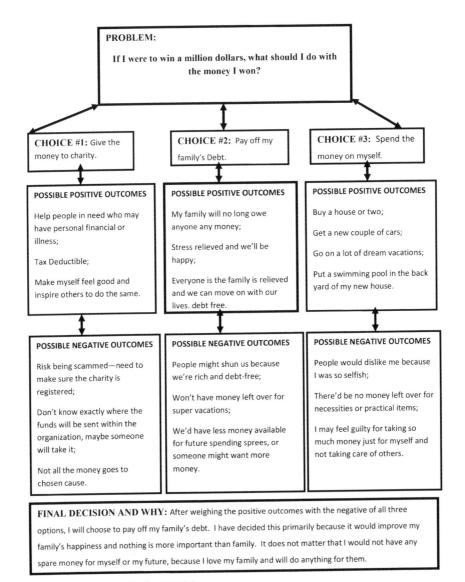

Figure 12.2.   James Black's DMGO

JOURNAL AND/OR DISCUSSION QUESTIONS

1. How do you suppose character education and/or development are connected to decision-making?
2. What is the format of the decision-making graphic organizer?
3. How do you suppose this DMGO might assist in decision-making or problem-solving?
4. If you were addressing the same decision as James, how might you solve that problem?
5. What was your response to James's final decision? Explain.

Chapter 13

Role-Play Scenarios for Enhancing Character Education's Decision-Making

CHAPTER OVERVIEW

The purpose of this chapter is to provide scenarios for the class to role-play or discuss. This could be considered a follow-up to chapter 12 on making a decision. The role-plays presented require decision-making for problem-solving along with reasoning applied to the acting-out of the scenario or the discussion/conversation about it.

These scenarios are most commonly nonscripted and call for an acting-out of the problem and supplying the solution. However, three formats for these scenarios are provided with the reasoning for each one given. Kinesthetic (whole-body) involvement is commonplace, but the other modalities of auditory, visual, and tactile are simultaneously present in this character-building interactive experience.

If you're in a classroom, then this role-playing may be done over several months or extended to doing one or two role-plays per week. If you're in a workshop on character education and development, it's suggested that the scenarios be done in small-group format. Each scenario is designed to address decision-making and/or problem-solving. The classroom community is built through sharing thoughts, ideas, opinions, and judgments. "Journal and/or Chapter Questions" end this chapter.

ADVANTAGES OF SCENARIO ROLE-PLAY

The first advantage of the role-play is to bring people together to face a problem that may not personally be part of their daily experience but is a part of our wider community or society's belief and value systems (see chapter 3).

For participants, their creativity and imagination are implemented during the role-play for finding a solution to a controversial situation. The cognitive skills of recognizing, realizing, comparing and contrasting, prioritizing, predicting, analyzing, evaluating, risk-taking, inventing, initial and advanced decision-making, recalling, and reflecting (see appendix A) are evidenced throughout the self-actualizing role-play activity.

SCENARIOS: FORMAT STYLE: PRESENTATION TOPIC: PURPOSE

1. *Format Style:* There are three format styles presented for this chapter's role-plays. One is not considered better than the others, but rather an opportunity for those involved to select a format best suited to the group or groups.;
2. *Presentation Topic:* The presentation topic is selected from a series listed and provided by the group leader of the workshop or classroom. The topics are controversial issues and considered common social cognition experiences. Additionally, the scenario topic is based on beliefs and values known to be shared by the groups participating as being an issue with which one might and then again might not agree.
3. *Purpose:* The purpose of the discussion groups or role-play ones is to bring about conversation *with* others that fosters reasoning. This in-depth thinking leads to a final decision when confronting a situation that is hypothetical, but may exist in schools or communities, as well as in a wider-based setting. Another purpose, as stated in the "Advantages of Scenario Role-Play" section is to address verbally cognitive skills and feelings surrounding a controversial situation. Using M. S. Schiering's (1999) *Reciprocal Thinking Skills Chart*, as seen in appendix A, these thinking skills include but are not exclusive to:

a. recognizing there is a problem and what it is;
b. realizing that the problem may be solved by talking with others and being involved in improvisational theater;
c. comparing and contrasting viewpoints and perspectives of those doing the role-play and later;
d. discussing the problem;
e. prioritizing the most plausible solutions to the problem presented;
f. predicting what's going to happen if different actions are taken;
g. analyzing those choices for possible positive and negative outcomes;

h. evaluating the actions, thoughts, ideas, and feelings of other group members and even the audience;

i. risk-taking with suggestions that may not meet the approval of the group;

j. inventing ways to problem-solve;

k. decision-making initially and at the advanced level when the role-play concludes and group and audience reactions are realized;

l. continually recalling and reflecting on past experiences and one's knowledge base about the role-play topic.

These thinking skills are evidenced throughout the self-actualizing role-play activity. Overall, "communication with others" is the key purpose.

Actual Scenario: There's "weed" to be shared. The setting is a summer day camp theater group's presentation on: *The Real World: To Meet or Not at 4:20.*

THREE POSSIBLE ROLE-PLAY FORMATS FOR PRESENTATION

The three possible role-play formats and the following "real-world" ones addressed are by husband and wife Josh and Katie Schiering (2014).

Format One: The scenario is written on a piece of paper and handed to a small group of three to five to hold a "discussion." Talking with one another is the key point of this group's function. A role-play might be seen as the group converses. This role-play is for the acting-out of how a decision is addressed. Those watching the role-play may comment when it's completed and offer other possible problem solutions.

Format Two: The role-play is presented to two small groups for an improvisational discussion role-play to be held to solve the assigned problem. Character names and actions might be part of the improvisation. Research may need to be conducted and a time lapse to use handheld devices is provided, as the group continues to talk. Talking may be partially interrupted, but the information presented for decision-making is ongoing, as Internet information is fed into the discussion.

The purpose of this format is oppositional, to have the role-play groups oppose one another's ideas and find solutions to the problem that fit in that environment and may be carried over to other places. Other groups watch this acted-out discussion and at the end may join in to offer thoughts, ideas, opinions, and feelings. Since stereotyping is commonplace, judgments may also be expressed.

Format Three: This role-play involves three groups which are titled "Good, Bad, and Ugly."

"For the 'good' group, a person comes into an already formed group and is offering 'weed/dube' to the group. The right way to deal with the problem is excluding this person from the group with members rejecting the offer. Case closed. The group has practiced being of good character, seeing the ramifications or some of them for such an action and how getting caught, let alone the moral decision, could have been escalated to take in family belief and values and, if caught, intensify, worsen, or heighten, and go downhill from there.

"In the 'Bad' group, one of the group members tells another he has 'weed' to share. They decide to take it and sneak off to the back of the building to try it. Crouching down low among 'soshing' commands when arriving there, they then get a little loud and obnoxious with laughing and pushing one another. Another group of kids comes around and seeing what's being denied them, they start a confrontation.

One member of the new group goes to find an adult on the other side of the building to tell about what's happening. In the few minutes that elapse, the noise becomes obvious to others nearby that something is going on, and a fight occurs between the two groups. The new onlookers are loud, and more attention is given so that now there are over twenty people involved and what was a small group has become loud and overbearing, as well as attracting attention from others nearby to see what's happening. What happens next is decided by all those in the role-play or watching it. Sidebar conversations follow along with whole-group problem-solving.

"The 'ugly' group has an older individual coming into it, and this person has a stash of different kinds of drugs he/she offers to each member to sell to others. 'Why should you be the only ones feeling good? And this way you can make some money. Take these home, and sell to other people, but not those right here. Every amount you sell, I'll pay you a good price. First try this one. It's a little different from 'weed' and is called ecstasy.

"There might actually be some laughing as the role plays are acted out, from what may be seen as the ridiculousness of the second and third role plays or how blunt and risky the actors are being. But, when things settle down, it's the designated role-play leaders' or observing and supervising individuals' role to point out how in 'real' life choosing may influence other decisions. Scenario two or three's solution to the problem, through inappropriate decision-making, makes the problem stay and possibly get worse. At some point, it's explained that the third role-play might well wind up with police being brought in, arrests being made, and jail time being served.

"The ramifications of jail time are then discussed, and the conversations within and between groups expands not just to that day, but go beyond it with information gathering from the internet concerning legal matters for selling drugs and getting caught. A time is set aside for large-group discussions, reinforcing the best of the three scenarios' decision-making and who were the protagonists and antagonists. The scenario presentation on a realistic situation brings the groups together to realize that decision- making by talking 'with' others can have a profound and positive impact once information is gathered and the parameters of being safe 'are' realized."

REAL-WORLD ROLE-PLAY INFORMATION

1. "The scenario about the 'weed' being available involved two groups. The first group serves as the supplier and the second group the recipients, with one group member threatening to 'rat out' the suppliers to a considered friendly camp counselor who'll be understanding. The counselor role, presented that way in the role-play, turns out not to be friendly, but confiscates the product. Where the situation goes from here involves the remainder of the role-play. Example: What's to be done with the counselor who now has the product? Does everyone keep quiet for fear of being caught, or does someone or the group go to a higher authority and report what happened?

2. "The scenario is written on a piece of paper, and three groups play out the *same* scene with each ones having a different response in the 'good,' the 'bad,' and the 'ugly' ways of the situation being addressed. This activity takes place at a summer day camp, and the activity, part of the theater group's project, is designed to address real situations that campers may encounter at school or in one's neighborhood. The role-plays are for future decision-making by being part of or watching what could happen. The first way is presented as it takes into consideration the 'right' way to solve the problem in accordance with good character traits evidenced and the major community's social cognition attitudes displayed.

3. "The second group purposefully does social cognition responses being the 'wrong' way because of consequences that may follow. The 'Ugly' group escalates the difficulties of the situation and not only doesn't solve the problem but also adds to it with ruining relationships, possibly police action having to be taken, or someone getting hurt, physically and/or emotionally.

4. "The reason for the last two presentation styles is for the groups to compare and contrast the means of handling the proposed problem with respect

to within and between scenarios. Additionally, it becomes evident that when the problem isn't handled properly, then other problems may be the result, which calls for more problem solving, discussion, and conversation to rectify the initial decision process not representing a person of good character."

A FEW OTHER SCENARIOS FOR ROLE-PLAY AND/OR DISCUSSION

Each scenario is designed to address a possibly controversial situation. How it's handled determines the conversations with one another as group members converse with one another to problem-solve similarly to the way done with the DMGO presented in chapter 12. The main objectives of these scenarios, as with decision-making and problem-solving are to have in-depth conversations with others that are ongoing. The conversations address character education and development.

ROLE-PLAY AND/OR DISCUSSION SCENARIOS

1. You're reading the last few pages of your book when you're interrupted by your friend. You want to finish the book, but your friend seems upset. You want to be there to help but want to see how the book ends right now. What do you say or do?
2. An eight-year-old overhears two of his "friends" talking about how he or she has two moms. What should the eight-year-old say or do?
3. Your mom says, "When I was your age I never . . . " What do you say or do?
4. Your cousin is visiting and goes to climb the tree in your neighbor's front yard. You think it's dangerous. What do you say or do?
5. Your teacher from last year sees you smoking cigarettes. You don't want anyone to know. What do you say or do?
6. You've been invited to a smashing party where you know there is going to be drinking and you want to go but think you shouldn't, especially since you're underage. What do you say or do when asked if you're going?
7. Your friend borrows your iPod and says it'll be returned in a few hours. It's been more than seven hours, your iPod is nowhere in sight, and neither is your friend calling you to say whaz-up. What do you do?
8. You go out for the day with a friend who becomes silent and gloomy and will not say what is wrong. What do you say or do?

9. Your friend, who does not know that you are listening to him or her on the phone, describes you as a _____. What do you say or do?

10. A person at a party which you are attending seems like he or she has had too much to drink. He or she keeps talking and won't leave you alone. What do you do?

11. A neighbor complains about how loud you're playing your car radio in the driveway, and you ignore this. What should you do to rectify your lack of consideration?

12. Your aunt who is taking care of you while your parents are away talks to you about how she thinks your parents are horrible at parenting, because they're too liberal. What do you say or do?

13. Your parents ask you how you'd feel if they adopted a little sister for you and you don't want that. But, you know they do want this. What do you say or do?

14. You are supposed to be babysitting your little brother who is thirteen, and you are seventeen. Your friend calls to say there's a party going on at his or her place and you need to be there. What do you do?

15. Your father brags about how good he was at sports when he was your age. How do you respond?

16. A member of your class opens her locker, and you see in it a few things you know have been lost by your friends. What do you say or do?

17. You know your best friend has had his first "joint," and you know this is causing problems. What do you say or do?

18. You want to be accepted by this group, but to be in it, you have to steal a book from a classmate. What do you say or do?

19. A friend constantly talks about money and the cost of things. What do you say or do to get him to stop?

20. You are twelve and you go shopping with your mother to buy clothes, but she wants to make all the choices for you. What do you say or do?

21. A family friend of your parents criticizes the way you look and makes some rather disgusting remarks about you and your friends. What do you say or do?

22. A teacher threatens to suspend you from school because he saw you bullying some kid in the lunchroom. What do you say or do?

23. A kid from your class harasses you all the time about coming to your house for a sleepover. What do you say or do?

24. A girl you know sometimes says the meanest things about you to someone you know from another class. What do you say or do?

25. You have reason to believe that this person from your class has posted terrible things about you on social media. What do you say or do?

26. The substitute teacher in your sixth-grade social studies class can't keep the class quiet. What do you say or do?

27. You suggest to a friend that you both go on the roller coaster ride at the amusement park, but you know she's scared. What do you say or do?
28. The gym teacher makes fun of you for finishing last in the race. What do you say or do?
29. Your grandparents are critical of the way you dress. What do you say?
30. You lent your friend your CD of your favorite singer, and he says it's lost. What do you say or do?
31. You get called to the principal's office because your teacher thinks you cheated on the last test when your score is higher than usual. But, you didn't cheat. What do you say or do?
32. You are seventeen and you're planning to go hiking with a few friends when your parents suddenly say, "No, you're not going." What do you say or do?
33. The person at the desk next to you is sniffing constantly, and it distracts you. What do you say or do?
34. You've been assigned a partner for the science project, and you'd prefer to work alone. What do you say to the teacher and/or the person with whom you're assigned to work?
35. You're in fourth grade, and you're going to have a birthday party. You think that it's right to invite all of the fourteen girls in your class to the party, but your mom has limited you to ten invites. What do you do?
36. You've studied for the chemistry test but know it's going to be really hard for you to pass it. The day of the test comes, and you need to decide whether to go to school or not. What do you do?

JOURNAL AND/OR DISCUSSION QUESTIONS

1. After examining the thirty-six possible scenarios, which three did you think might be most meaningful for:

    a. first through fifth graders;
    b. sixth through eighth graders;
    c. adolescents;
    d. young Adults;
    e. middle-agers;
    f. seniors?

2. Would you rather be the observer of a role-play or the one doing the acting? Why do you suppose you gave that answer?
3. Did any of the scenarios leave you "stuck?" How could you develop your critical thinking?

Chapter 14

Inappropriate Behavior: An Intervention Program

Angela Sullivan

CHAPTER OVERVIEW

In the preceding chapters there have been thirteen different topics relating to character education and its development. Nearly every chapter has one or two activities to support the chapter's theme information. These personality awareness activities have been suggested for use in a classroom or workshop at the K-16+ grade levels, and when applicable where one works or resides. Each chapter provides different approaches to character education, and its accompanying development and/or components of such programs.

To add another element to the idea of what it is to be a person of good character, Angela Sullivan, EdD, a former vice principal living in the Hudson Valley of New York, explains about a program at her Thiells Elementary school in Rockland County, NY, from 2005 through spring of 2014. This program deals with intervention measures when behavior is inappropriate and/or the elementary students were not persons of good character.

Dr. Sullivan explains that some of the material in this chapter came from personal experiences with committee work on the federally imposed Response to Intervention and Positive Behavior Intervention Support (PBIS) programs. She references two works for her research on this being Kerr and Nelson (2010) and, before that, Kaplan and Carter in 1995, with respect to strategies for managerially handling the behavior problems of those in a social setting. She explains the meaning and necessity of having a character education and development program in place in each class-room by establishing the school's *code of conduct* and having a *matrix of behaviors*.

POSITIVE BEHAVIOR INTERVENTION SUPPORT

"In our elementary school, we wanted a program that our students could buy into with respect to realizing the importance of having an appropriate behavior code or set of rules.

"From my experience, in traditional education, a punishment system was in-place for those who misbehaved. If a student did something like cheat on a test, throw paper on the floor, or say something that wasn't appropriate, then consequences were established and implemented.

"Each infraction had a correspondingly established punishment for those who 'disobeyed' the school rules, but often different children received different punishments. Perhaps recess was taken away, or a student was sent to the school principal for a reprimand. Being chastised in front of classmates was rather commonplace in educational settings, and this was the case for many decades. The basic result was that children felt uncomfortable, and those 'troublemakers' were either peer-revered and/or a fear of them was the operative. It wasn't enough to fear the unknown; now with bullying truly present, there was a direct object for concerns.

"Basically, the 'fear' idea didn't work for promoting positive behaviors in the school's classrooms. There was an advantage for the one doing the bullying or breaking the rules, as this person got a good deal of attention. One student said, 'Having classmates or schoolmates being afraid of me was rather cool.' He continued, "Yeah, I got a lot of negative attention, true, but I was still being noticed.'

"Of course, being afraid of the school bullies wasn't good for the well-behaved students. One student said, 'There I was being really good in the classroom and basically I was ignored by the teacher and everyone else, while the one in trouble was getting a lot of attention.'

"This idea of character education needed to be incorporated school-wide. PBIS provided a proactive and interactive approach to establish a social culture in a school that supported social, emotional, and academic success. It is aimed at sustaining safe and effective school environments while preventing behavior problems with students."

Levels of Intervention

"Paraphrased from this chapter's 'Chapter Overview,' the references for this section were used to explain an ongoing type of framework to target practices and interventions based on the level of supports that individual students need. These include intervention at primary, secondary, and tertiary levels. Each one progresses gradationally, with more intensive services given to those who engage in high-at-risk behaviors, or are in specialized groups, or require individualized attention. This is because of the inappropriate behavioral level's being in high excess of what's considered acceptable in the school.

"The important component of our school's behavioral intervention program was the team collaboration approach. This is where every faculty member had to buy-into the program and 'establish a data-based framework' for decision-making regarding behaviors that were permissible and those that were not. Other factors for the team were to establish the same punishment for certain behaviors and additionally create a reward system.

"Hopefully, over the long run, this reward system would not be materialistic, but intrinsically-based; meaning the students behaved well because they wanted to do that, as opposed to receiving a sticker or such, for good behavior. Of course, rewards were established by expectations and rules established for the school, and they came with 'monitoring, in the classroom, students' actions, as well as evaluating them.' Consequences were also put-in-place for those not following the school-wide behavior plan."

Code of Conduct for Students and Teachers

"A school-wide 'Code of Conduct' was set-in-place and included four statements beginning with 'I am.' The statements ended with one of the following to total four statements: respectful, responsible, safe, and prepared. It was realized by the collaborating team that having a school functioning best meant one that addressed these statements being practiced by students and teachers alike.

"A student who thought there was nothing 'in it' for him to be 'good' realized there was something of value, if only feeling good was the result. The six international traits of a person of good character, presented in chapter 1 of this book, were emphasized. Reiterated, these include one's being respectful, caring, fair, trustworthy, responsible, and a good citizen. Of course, these behaviors must be practiced in school and at any related school function or on the school bus if used by the students. Practicing them each day regardless of the location was seen as a possible outgrowth of the positive behavior concept."

How Proper Behaviors Were Taught

"Proper behaviors were taught by addressing what's seen in this book's appendix B, and in the individual chapters 1–9. Additionally, the character development workshop that has been mentioned in this book along with classroom activities presented there is being used to emphasize concepts or emphasizing positive behaviors. Furthermore, in this book there have been role-plays, discussions, and integral conversations. All of these are the same or similar to what we did in Thiells Elementary school in Rockland County, NY, with praise for good behavior, training for teachers and parents, and having a 'cooldown time' when/if things got out of hand. Flexibility was also an important component of our behavior program. Frankly, if some punishment, or reward, or activity was not deemed effective, then alternative strategies were discussed, decided upon, and implemented."

"BE A STAR" MATRIX

The PBIS team with Dr. Sullivan created a "Be a Star" Matrix. This is seen in figure 14.1.

"BE A STAR" MATRIX
BE a STAR!

	Cafeteria	Hallway	Playground	Bathroom	Bus
Safety	1. Keep hands, feet, and objects to yourself. 2. Always walk to from your table. 3. Stay seated at your assigned seat.	1. Keep hands, feet, and objects to yourself. 2. Walk. 3. Stay in line facing forward.	1. Keep hands, feet, and objects to yourself. 2. Use equipment appropriately.	1. Keep hands, feet, and objects to yourself. 2. Flush and wash your hands. 3. When finished, return to where you need to be.	1. Keep hands, feet, and objects to yourself. 2. Walk. 3. Stay seated facing forward. 4. Keep the aisle clear.
Teamwork	1. Use voice level 2. 2. Clean up your area.	1. Use voice level 0.	1. Share. 2. Play by the rules.	1. Use voice level 1. 2. Place used paper towels in the trash.	1. Use voice level 2. 2. Pick up trash in and around your seat.
Attitude	1. Say "please" and "thank you." 2. Wait your turn.	1. Accept directions without arguing or complaining. 2. Greet others with a smile.	1. Take turns. 2. Be a good sport. 3. Invite others to join a game.	1. Wait your turn.	1. Greet your driver with a smile. 2. Take turns getting on and off the bus. 3. Share your seat.
Respect	1. Follow directions of cafeteria staff and monitors. 2. Use kind words. 3. Only touch your own food.	1. Follow directions. 2. Use kind words.	1. Follow directions. 2. Use kind words.	1. Use kind words. 2. Stay away from occupied stalls.	1. Follow directions. 2. Use kind words.

Voice levels

0 = silence

1 = only the person next to you can hear you

2 = the people at your table can hear

3 = outside voices

Figure 14.1.   Be a Star Matrix

JOURNAL AND/OR DISCUSSION QUESTIONS

1. In your own words, how would you describe the RTI (Response to Intervention) and PBIS programs?
2. What are your opinions (give at least three) on the "Be a Star" Matrix created by the teachers in Dr. Sullivan's elementary school?

Chapter 15

Book Activity and Four Life Statements for Daily Living

CHAPTER OVERVIEW

A list of fifty-three books and each one's author or authors are provided in appendix B. However, the activity for using those books or ones of your choosing is presented at the start of this chapter. Each book listed in appendix B has a moral or ethical message serving as the story's resolution. The books, although considered pieces of children's literature, have relevance for those of any age, as the topics are applicable, pertinent, and appropriately significant concerning character education and development.

The activity involving the book reading is followed by Four Statements/ Rules for Everyday Happiness in a way that being a person of good character is obvious. "Journal and/or Discussion Questions" end the chapter.

BOOKS: CHILDREN'S LITERATURE

Books, whether for children or at a higher reading level, have four major components. These include the rising action, climatic point, descending action, and story resolution. In order to have these sections, the story has six elements. These are the characters, setting, moods, events, problem, and solution. In some books, the writer's message is clear and overt, and in other writings this message is more subliminal. With this information in mind, this activity first involves students and/or workshop attendees reading the books orally to one another. While this oral reading may be an experience not had for some time by workshop attendees, there are reasons for this listed under "Activity Purpose."

Activity Purpose

The reasons for this activity are:

1. Oral reading stimulates communication.
2. Reader-to-reader and then whole-group collaboration is observed in this activity.
3. The fact that there are social experiences and issues that are universal concerning being a person of good character is recognized.
4. There are common issues that are part of social cognition and universal social daily experiences.
5. There's nearly always a decision to be made, and when reading aloud with another, that sharing of the correctness of the decision may be finitely examined.
6. The overall message in the book is one that reiterates, in some manner, the idea of moral decisions that require one's attention is being focused on being a person of good character.

"Ethical issues may also be addressed, and certainly there are decisions to be made and meaning to be received regarding these issues. Once the aforementioned six purposes are accomplished, there is the idea of sharing the books until each is read by each member of the class or workshop assemblage."

Activity Directions

Select a book from those listed in appendix B. Or have at least fifteen books at the ready for an oral reading in partnerships. The book must be on the topic of character development, a moral issue, or the subject and importance of beliefs through one's values. After reading the book aloud to a partner, have a chart paper available to list the book's title and main message the book's readers think was provided.

When these have been recorded on the chart paper or papers, go over them orally with the entire assemblage. Then, either now or later, do over the process until all the books are read and discussions on the topics of them have been held. This activity may take several weeks to complete, as reading one book a week is suggested, as opposed to reading many books in one day or in one week. Figure 15.1 gives examples of how this activity looks when completed.

CLASSROOM, HOME, OR CHARACTER EDUCATION WORKSHOP ACTIVITY: ORAL READING AND BOOK'S TITLE AND MESSAGE IDENTIFICATION CHART

ABOUT THE BOOK + AUTHOR'S NAME	BOOK'S MESSAGES
1. The Three Questions By Jon J. Muth, adapted from Leo Tolstoy's story in 1906 When is the best time to do thing? Who is the most important one? What is the right thing to do?	1. The most important time is now = seize the moment. The most important one is who's by your side being supportive. And if you're alone, then you're the most important one. Lastly, the right thing to do is to do good deeds for others. These three questions and answers are why we're here.
2. Sammy Snail's A Time for Quiet By M. S. Schiering A snail is personified and goes around asking other animals how to reduce noise pollution.	2. We all need a little time for quiet in our day to reflect and relax. Mindfulness is the key to being a stress reducer.
3. Hey Little Ant By Phillip and Hannah Hoose A boy is deciding whether to step on an ant and says since he's big and his friends agree he should step on the ant. The ant pleads his case saying that it's important to its colony of ants.	3. The bully needs to look at the feelings of the one being bullied. The story's end doesn't have a resolution, but asks the reader to decide if the boy should step on the ant. This is a decision-making book that leads one to think bullying is not okay.

Figure 15.1. Three Books and Their Messages

FOUR STATEMENTS/RULES FOR EVERYDAY HAPPINESS

The statements provided in this section are those used these past eighteen years in this author's college courses and, before that, in career-sequential teaching of grades five, three, one, and six. The idea became life lessons and the fiber or key concepts of these environments. Statement one went school-wide in the latter part of the 1970s. Who knows where this one has traveled these past decades? The author has been told by former teacher candidates that it is the one rule they put in their classroom, as it brings unity, a sense of purpose, and good community feelings to their shared environment. Each forthcoming statement has a little introduction and then is stated in large bold print.

However, before reading these statements or life lessons being part of *your* life, you're invited to think about the following quotation:

> "Regardless of one's age, gender, ethnicity, cultural mores, race, religion, level of education, or title, there are two types of people in the world. These are those who are kind and those who are unkind.
>   The first have substance and value . . . the latter do not." (M. S. Schiering 1967)

Now, the Statements

Statement # 1: This idea addresses a way to conduct yourself that serves a purpose of having not only good feelings and thoughts about yourself but also for others as well. Incorporating this rule and realizing that one feels good about himself or herself by using it results in the classroom environment, place where one works, or home being a comfort zone, a congenial place where one's safety predominates. That is because, when the rule is active, there is no negativity present and positivity rules! M.S. Schiering (1976, 2015, 2016 b and c) stated the first rule and it is:

"*No* Put-Downs . . . *Only* Lift-Ups!"

Statement # 2: This idea addresses the concept that sometimes, when an individual is in a place that is new to him or her, that gathering place need not be feared. Each of us in that location has first a sense of self-acceptance by following statement # 1. Certainly, the place where one is doesn't matter so much as the attitude when there. Therefore, statement # 2, stated by Million in 1990, is:

"I belong everywhere!"

Statement # 3: This idea addresses the purpose of our lives, the reason we are here, and the focus of one's attention about daily living. This idea was developed by this book's author in 2003. It came about when she was walking into a course where she was the professor. She felt she shared the teaching and learning with those in that college classroom. For that matter, the whole college, community, or place where she was or would be going was a shared environment. These following words came to mind, and have been shared ever since then. The statement is:

"Wherever you go, instead of saying to yourself:

1. What's in this for me?
   . . . . .Or. . . . .

2. *What am I getting from this?*
. . . . *Say.* . . . .
What may I give to this experience?

Statement # 4: This idea addresses the concept of not forgetting what someone did that was hurtful but forgiving someone for what he or she said or did. Next there is the realization that our life is not for getting things but for giving them. The statement is:

Our life is not forgetting but forgiving.
Our life is not for getting but for giving!

JOURNAL AND/OR DISCUSSION QUESTIONS

1. What is your opinion of the book reading activity? Why do you suppose you have that answer?
2. Which of the four statements resonate with you and why?

Chapter 16

Self-Acceptance: I Am Enough: Two Stories for Character Development

CHAPTER OVERVIEW

The author provides some thoughts on what is meant by self-acceptance. Then, the concept of one's being *enough* is given attention. This concept is followed by addressing comparing and contrasting and things being the way they are. Two stories follow: the first one about a world history class and the second about a big and little tree in a forest. These are titled *Being Enough: Story One* and *Two*.

Both of these stories have been told by the author for decades to address the topic of character development. The stories collectively serve as object lessons. The first story deals with how believing in oneself can change a person's image from negative to positive. The second story deals with the concept of a person's being *enough* as he or she is: self-acceptance. The chapter concludes with a reflection, "Journal and/or Discussion Questions," "Author's Culminating Comments," and a poem from 1896.

SELF-ACCEPTANCE CONCEPT AND TEACHING FOR CHARACTER DEVELOPMENT

Character development addresses having personality traits that are amenable. These traits stem from one's thinking well of himself or herself. The concept of accepting oneself because of the way one behaves leads to self-respect. Self-respect can be given to others. As stated in a previous chapter, "You can give to another only that which you first have for yourself" (S.D. Schiering 1999). Subsequently, of major importance in character education and development is teaching self-acceptance and the idea of one's being "enough!"

A Look at Self-Acceptance

I wonder what comes to your mind when you read the words "self-acceptance?" Are you ever enough, or do you have the sense of being enough? Do you criticize yourself, and do you practice positive self-talk as explained in chapter 4's activity "What's Right with You?"

Truth be known, we live in a world society that emphasizes what's wrong with everyone, with you, me, anybody. For the most part, self-esteem or acceptance doesn't rely on where you live or the things you have. It seems that there is always negativism at hand or close at hand. Why? Why is so much time spent with lack of self-acceptance and, in-turn, self-worth or confidence in what one says or does?

Maybe the answer lies in a pattern's having been set and that's just the way it is. Maybe during the growing-up years at home or school when we received criticism for something, as years passed we spent a lifetime focused on how we constantly fell short of some overtly or subconsciously designated mark. Subsequently, we acknowledged ourselves as a failure.

Improving or doing better wasn't addressed. Then again, maybe the criticism caused one to examine himself or herself and strive to do better. Well, there's basically nothing wrong with that "improvement" idea, as one comes to appreciate his or her qualities, behaviors, and character traits that are honorable.

Comparing and Contrasting

The beginning awareness cognitive skills of finding similarities between ourselves and others are woven into our daily lives. This is whether at school or home, on a vacation, or at a friend's house. The location doesn't matter, what does matter is that comparing and contrasting ourselves to those we know and even strangers is continually done. Noting likenesses or differences is ongoing, if not in your consciousness then just under the radar.

What is compared and contrasted? There are a multitude of answers to that question, but each example addresses what was better than or less than, as opposed to equality being evidenced. For example, this author always wanted to be like her sister who was ten years older than she. Her sister was tall and willowy, while this author was short and rather large. Her dad promised her that she'd be tall and willowy one day, but she wanted that right now.

Another more general comparison point may be that a person wasn't as good at reading as others in school, or reading came later than the accepted "norm" of age five or six, kindergarten or first grade. Or, perhaps one person was not as good at a particular sport that was recognized as being important. Then again, perhaps test scores were compared, and some were the top students and others "not so bright." Whatever the point of comparison, it usually took only one "less than" to have a sense of not being enough or inadequacy, a lack of self-worth resulting in no or minimal self-acceptance.

That inadequacy, marginalized as it may be, stood out for the one who felt it. The person in question and it may be you, started to have a self-image that was lacking in self-esteem, because of a sense of defectiveness. And that is where this lack of self-esteem, worthiness, valuing issue has its foundation, in a sense of insufficiency. Individuals come to recognize not being enough. To be such seems to be impossible, but that's the way it is.

The Way It Is

If it's just "the way it is" with respect to not giving attention to self-acceptance or valuing your "being a person of good character," because it is "just the way it is," then how does that change? Does someone we like or maybe even don't know need to tell us our worth in order to determine it? Maybe, yes. Does that deliverer of information need to be someone who's world known, a community member, a sibling, a parent, or someone of importance to you? Hmmm, that's an interesting question for discussion and/or reflection.

Being Enough: Example

As stated before, thinking "one is enough" is unlikely, for the most part, because of comparing and contrasting ourselves to others and coming up short. Perhaps to have full comprehension of this idea one needs to have an understanding of what it is to feel worthy. Being accepting of self has its foundation in a sense of self-valuing. Let's say it's your birthday and you anticipate and get a gift. Your thinking may be that getting a present is deserved because you are a thoughtful person and value yourself and think others do as well.

Then again, the gift giver person may see you as being worthy of getting a gift. Then again, Amy Meyers (2017d) suggests that maybe the gift giving has to do with one's level of thoughtfulness for another or perhaps it's just a ritual of the gift giver. In that case, the valuing is simply a characteristic of the one giving the gift. Still, whatever the reason there is one person having a sense of worthiness for self or another.

Being Enough: Story One

Some time ago, I heard of a tenth-grade world history teacher assigning a class-reading of textbook pages to help prepare them for a test on Charlemagne. A student in the class who was an excellent listener and participator in class discussions read those pages and wondered why this first Holy Roman emperor wasn't mentioned on those pages. The girl called her friend and asked if pages 154–167 were the ones she read, and her straight "A" friend replied that those were the pages she'd read to prepare for the test.

The next day, the test was given and the girl didn't think she'd done well but put her name on the test and answered the questions. The following day, the test came back, and the student had a "3" as her score. The teacher, an elderly bluish-white–haired woman, came by her desk and asked, "Why didn't you read those pages?" The girl replied that she had, but there was nothing about "Charlemagne" on them. The teacher replied, "Open your book and read the first sentences." The student read, "Charlie Magknee was a great leader."

The teacher instructed her not to read anymore sentences and told her how proud of her she was because she shared in class and participated so well and was a good listener. She explained how she showed reasoning and discernment and that she was so bright. The girl said, "You've the wrong person, you must mean my friend, but not me."

The teacher replied, this author was told, with words that changed her life. She said, "You pronounced the name Charlemagne incorrectly and that's why you didn't do well on the test. You kept looking for the name and got caught up in the mispronunciation by saying Charlie Magknee. However, there are many things you do well, like being that good listener and participating, which I mentioned before. Listen, I have something to say to you. *I believe in you.* Next time, if you're having trouble, come see me, I'm here to help." The girl thought, "If she can believe in me, maybe I can believe in myself."

Valuing and believing in someone can change one's personal perspective. Maybe now and then there is a person who's a catalyst for one's having high self-esteem. If you have it, you can give it to another. You can share this part of character education in a way that acknowledges the positives of another. Then, that person can do such for himself or herself and pass it along.

Being Enough: Story Two: Clarifying Self-Worth

(The following story is one this author has told for many decades. She no longer remembers where she first heard it or who told it. Maybe it was a conglomeration of stories she'd heard at one time or another that had significance for her. Looking up the story on the Internet she found it nowhere, at least not in this forthcoming version).

Once upon a time far away and long ago, there was a small tree and a large one standing beside one another on the front line of a forest. Hundreds of trees were alongside them. About a thousand were behind them. They looked no different from any of the other trees, except for the difference in their size. In front of them was a large spacious field, and at one end was a hill. Beyond the field were houses of all shapes and sizes, a community.

It was the winter, and snow covered the ground. Children on sleds, snow saucers, toboggans, and pieces of plastic went to the top of the hill and slid down it. Screaming with excitement, they ended their ride at the bottom of the hill right in front of the trees. They used the little tree as a turnaround.

With one hand gripping the sled rope and the other touching the tree, they went behind it back up the hill to slide down it again. Each day, throughout this cold and chilly season, when the children left and the little tree stood beside the big one, it said to its neighbor, "I wish I were big and tall like you and my branches touched the stars."

The big tree, throughout the season, responded with, "Don't you see how you're the turnaround point for the children? You are so important. Besides, one day you'll be big and tall like me and your branches will touch the stars." The little tree said, "I know, but I want to be big and tall like you and have my branches touch the stars, now." The big tree said nothing more.

The springtime came, and all over the little tree there were pink flowers. The fragrance of them was delightful and filled the air. The children came to the little tree and getting a boost-up or being tall enough they climbed the little tree and smelled the flowers, excitedly.

Every day it was the same, and at the end of the day when the children had gone to their houses, the little tree turned to the big tree and said, "I wish I was big and tall like you and my branches touched the stars." The big tree, throughout the season, responded with, "Didn't you see how the children climbed up your trunk and smelled your flowers? I don't even have flowers. You are so special. Besides, one day you'll be big and tall like me and your branches will touch the stars." "I know" said the little tree, "but I want to be big and tall and have my branches touch the stars, now."

The springtime turned to summer and the little tree was full of green leaves as was the big tree. The children came with friends and parents to picnic in the field in front of the trees. The children played tag and the little tree was home base. Some children climbed into the little tree and swung from its branches. One little girl climbed into the little tree and looked out to the houses saying, "I can see forever from here."

A boy brought his book and sat on one of the little tree's branches and read for hours. At the end of the day, the boy's mother called him to come down from the tree and he responded, "I could just stay here and read." He was so content to sit in the little tree and be by himself, relaxed and enjoying his book.

When the end of the day had come and the children were in their houses, the little tree turned to the big tree and said, "I wish I were big and tall like you and my branches touched the stars." The big tree responded with, "Didn't you see how you were home base for the game of tag that the children played? Didn't you see the child climb into your branches and look at all that lay before her? Didn't you see that boy reading in your branches and not wanting to go home? You are so valued. Besides, one day you'll be big and tall like me and your branches will touch the stars." "I know" said the little tree, "but I want to be big and tall and have my branches touch the stars, now."

The fall came, and all over the little tree round red apples appeared. The children climbed the little tree and took the apples and put them in bags to take home where they were used to make applesauce, butter, pie, juice, cake, bread, and turnovers. Some children ate the apples from the tree as they plucked one off, standing under the tree's protective branches. This happened for weeks, and each day when the children left, the little tree turned to the big tree and said, "I wish I were big and tall like you and my branches touched the stars."

The big tree said, "Didn't you see that you have provided apples for the children? Do you realize that some ate the apples and others took them home to make delicious foods with them? Do you know that you provided sustenance? You are so amazing! You're a gift to the forest."

Then, just as the big tree was about to say, "Besides, one day you'll be big and tall like me and . . ." There was one last apple on the tree. At this moment it fell to the ground. When it hit the ground, it was on its side. It split in half. Looking at the apple the big tree finished its sentence with, "you don't have to be concerned about being big and tall like me and your branches touching the stars, because the stars are inside you. You are enough just the way you are." (See figure 16.1.)

Figure 16.1. The Stars are Inside Us

The Story's End

The storyteller cuts the apple in half and reveals the star in this apple. Also, a sliver is cut off and placed against a dark surface (see figure 16.1) so the "star" may be easily seen. Then, it's explained that when cutting the apple in half this way, all apples have the star shape. The color or type of apple does not matter. The storyteller adds, "And so it is with each of us. The stars are inside, and we just need to acknowledge their being there and realize our worth. I am enough, and so are you."

Reflection

These two stories have been part of this author's way of addressing self-acceptance. Having positive self-esteem and feeling more than adequate and definitely worthy of noting personality traits that equate with being a person of good character are mainstays. There are people who will always put you down, but that doesn't mean you need to do this to yourself. Why should you? There's no purpose.

When telling the first story in middle-school grades and college, the reaction with the mispronunciation of the emperor's name brings laughter. But, the message of the story with the words "I believe in you," seems to captivate the listener's attention and thinking about how these four words can impact a person's self-perception.

The second story has been told to first, third, fifth, and sixth graders, as well as college classes. The response, when the apple is cut in half, is always the same. There is a wonderment facial expression. There is a sigh, which signifies a realization of comparing one's self to the star in the apple; accepting oneself as being special. The stars are on the inside and being oneself, a person of good character, equates with self-valuing and worthiness.

JOURNAL AND/OR DISCUSSION QUESTIONS

1. What do you think is meant by self-acceptance and being enough?
2. Have you ever compared yourself to someone else? If so, who was that? What quality or qualities did you want to have that you thought you didn't possess? Why?
3. What does it mean to *model* being a person of good character?
4. What was your overall opinion about the first and then second story? Why do you suppose you have these reactions?
5. What is the message of this chapter?

AUTHOR'S CULMINATING COMMENTS

This book has been written to bring forth ideas concerning character education and development with respect to being persons of good character at school, the workplace, home and everywhere. The chapter topics and activities have addressed the overall theme of this book with respect to making one's environment, regardless of where it is, a pleasant place of harmony. How to accomplish that has been the main theme of every idea presented on these pages. What it all comes down to is our world, which is in the poem by the same title, written by A. D. Walton in 1896. It reads as follows:

> *Our World*
> *We make the world in which we live*
> *By what we gather and what we give*
> *By our daily deeds and the things we say*
> *By what we keep or cast away . . .*
> *We make our world by the life we lead,*
> *By the friends we have, by the books we read,*
> *By the pity we show in the hour of care,*
> *By the loads we lift and the love we share.*
> *We make our world by the goals we pursue,*
> *By the heights we seek and the higher view,*
> *By the hopes and the dreams that reach the sun,*
> *And a will to fight till the heights are won.*
> *We gather . . . We scatter . . . We take and we give . . .*
> *We make this world, and here we live.*

You are invited to make our schools, classrooms, communities, world, and especially homes comfortable places by practicing, teaching, and modeling being persons of good character.

Afterword

This Teacher's Reflection: M. S. Schiering (1998)

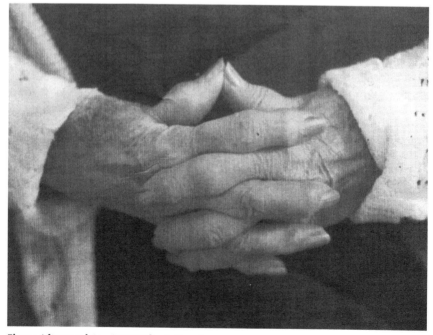

Figure Afterword 1:   My Mother's Hands

"These are my mother's hands. They are flecked with age spots and gnarled from years of arthritis. At nearly ninety-two years in 1998 these hands had experienced a great deal. They'd travelled as far away as China and spent a lifetime visiting sisters and brothers all over the United States. Also, they spent at least half a lifetime helping raise my siblings and me.

"I remember these hands stroking my head in the fourth grade when I was so upset that the teacher didn't call on me to answer a question, for over three months. I remember these hands, freshly manicured in bright pink polish, helping me back onto my fat-wheeled, green tricycle when I'd fallen off it. I remember them braiding my hair until I was ten. It was then that I took up a pair of scissors and decided to give myself my first haircut. And I remember, on that occasion, those very same hands wiping away my tears while gently consoling me with: 'You're right. Your classmate, Amy, does look pretty in short hair. So, I guess it was a reasonable decision to cut off your own. Anyway, it will grow back.' When I finally stopped crying, she added, 'Sweetheart, this too shall pass.'"

"I remember those normally very consoling hands with the right one extended and slapping my face when I cursed for the first time, because I couldn't fit into my cousin Sue's dress for the sixth-grade dance. I remember these hands tightly gripping mine at picnics or when strolling along the lakefront beach. And I could never forget an index finger pointing in my direction, shaking up and down, accompanied by angry words when I was testing my independence during adolescence.

"I remember those hands touching my sister's cheek when she got married, and I remember a few years later, their reluctance to let my brother go when she thought he'd be drafted into the army. I remember their endless grips on various golf clubs followed by a statement like "I'll never get this right!" Sometimes the same was said when she went bowling and played various card games.

"These hands were congratulatory when I rode my first horse, passed my state exams, and graduated high school at age eighteen. And, nearly twenty years later I stroked these hands when my father died. It was then that I helped my mother get through the first summer without her fifty year lifemate. However, amidst all this, I also remember the first day she sent me off to school and put me in the care of someone else's hands.

"Every day from either mid-August or early September, parents put their most precious gifts, their children, into the teacher's hands. Hence, over the years, between eight to ten, thirty to thirty-five hours during the school week, we are the caretakers. What we do with those precious gifts, those children of others, whether they are in elementary school, middle or high school, college or beyond, they are someone else's children. It is our responsibility to guide with compassion, model what it is to be a person of good character, and demonstrate conversing and sharing. Maybe in the process we come to appreciate ourselves and others."

Appendixes Overview

There are five appendices (A–E) in this book. These are presented to add to the book's chapters and/or offer clarification of the chapters.

A: Reciprocal Thinking Skills Chart (with twenty-six cognitive and/or meta-cognitive skills definitions)
B: Books with Moral Messages Activity
C: Character Development Activities: Sequence of Presentation
D: Causes and Possible Prevention of Bullying, Harassment, Discrimination, and Prejudice
E: Post–Character Development Workshop: Three Reflections

Appendix A

Reciprocal Thinking Phases: Cognition and Meta-cognition

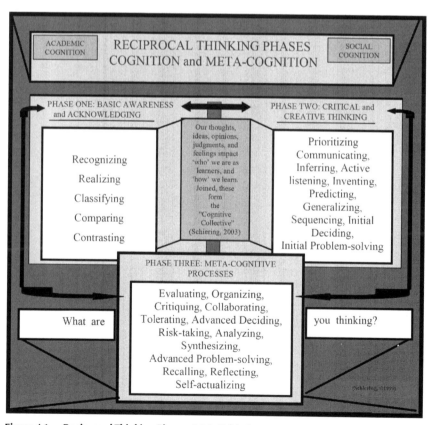

Figure A1. Reciprocal Thinking Phases (M.S. Schiering 1999, 2003, 2011, 2015, 2016a)

In chapter 3, the Reciprocal Thinking Phases section is the cognitive collective and is mentioned as the core of the social cognition model. In that place it's described as being a combination of thinking and feeling. The interplay between thoughts, ideas, opinions, judgments, and emotional reactions to situations is addressed. This portion of the book explains that thinking and feeling are reciprocal processes. Reciprocity means that there's movement between and among what one is thinking and what one is feeling, as much as there's reciprocity between each of these, individually. Each impacts the other, and cognitive function moves simultaneously through and around these thinking phases.

Thinking and Feeling Woven Together

Thinking and feeling are so closely woven together that it's oftentimes difficult to distinguish one from the other, as they impact what's said or done. The interactions of these two shape the dynamics of the classroom and the likelihood that students will achieve the desired learning outcome. Figure A1, which appears at the beginning of this appendix, particularly addresses three phases of thinking, and these are beginning awareness and acknowledging, critical and creative thinking, and the metacognitive processes. The reciprocity of thinking as well as feelings refers to the ongoing exchange of comprehension that forms memory. Memory and the reflection involved with it result in impacting how one may react to a new situation in a social or academic setting by relying on previous experiences.

Example: The professor brought snacks to class and this was remembered by a few students who no longer were in this class a few semesters later. They stopped by the room that this professor was in to see if they could get some snacks. They did this because they were hungry and recalled this unusual accommodation or consideration of the professor bringing snacks to class, most fondly. They remembered the class, feelings it had engendered, the snacks being a feel-good situation, and now a means to satisfy their hunger needs.

Cognitive Collective: A Few More Thoughts

Bogner in (2011c) explains that "human beings think as well as feel. The result is that this unity of thinking and feeling happens within the classroom, as well as outside it. Throughout a person's day, individuals move between varying cognitive processes and emotions. As character development is addressed, we must recognize this natural progression and interplay by noticing, first, that they occur, and, second, that in order to be effective teachers or human beings, we must know how this process happens and attend to it."

This exchange occurs within and between the phases of beginning awareness, critical and creative thinking, and the metacognitive processes.

What one is thinking may not be what I am thinking, but awareness of what is transpiring cognitively empowers learners and teachers alike. This empowerment happens while providing self-efficacy. Knowing what one is thinking helps to clarify learning with the individual's acknowledging the finite identification of the cognitive and metacognitive processes being experienced at any time along with emotions that result from or are intertwined with the thinking skills. Certain thinking skills trigger varying emotions.

AN EXAMPLE OF CONNECTING THINKING AND FEELINGS

For example, if I am comparing and contrasting while simultaneously forming an opinion about someone's participation in the class, I may recognize that I didn't have that awareness, and feel a sense of inadequacy. Or the opposite of that might happen, and I feel elated. Regardless, the reaction I experience is due to the cognitive skill that's identified.

Definition of Reciprocal Thinking Skills

Looking at figure A1 the thinking skills addressed in each phase can be read and realized that while in a phase they are still addressed, thinking wise, in a simultaneous manner. It's very important to realize that each thinking skill may be addressed reciprocally for any situation. Therefore, it's understood that reciprocal thinking is not done sequentially, as an individual may move within and between phases at the same moment. One may be realizing at the same instant he or she is comparing, evaluating, or prioritizing, which are skills represented in each of the phases and not moving form phase one to two to three. Most important is realizing that there is no order when reciprocity is evidenced. The thinking skills within each phase are defined as follows.

PHASE 1: BEGINNING AWARENESS AND ACKNOWLEDGING

1. Recognizing: To be aware of, be familiar with, acknowledge, or identify from previous experience.
2. Realizing: To become conscious of something or comprehend it.
3. Classifying: To arrange, sort or order things into groups according to established criteria.
4. Comparing: To examine, judge, link, or evaluate two or more things in order to show how they are similar.

5. Contrasting: To show the difference, distinction, or disparity between two things being compared.

PHASE 2: CRITICAL AND CREATIVE THINKING

1. Prioritizing: To deal with or list something in order of its importance or level of concern.
2. Communicating: To converse in oral, written, or sign formats—a means for sharing, making a statement, passing along information, or publicizing.
3. Inferring: To suppose, deduce, surmise, and/or form an opinion based on the information one has.
4. Active listening: To be engaged in hearing what is being related by being attentive to the discourse.
5. Inventing: To discover, think up, devise, or fabricate in the mind, to think out, produce something new, or organize through experiment.
6. Predicting: To forecast, envision, guess, and/or calculate that something will happen before it actually occurs.
7. Generalizing: To form an opinion or take a broad view of something.
8. Sequencing: A series of related events, actions, or the like that happen or are done in a particular order/progression—placing in specific order.
9. Initial deciding: Beginning choice, resolution, or judgment about something as in making up one's mind concerning how to handle a situation.
10. Initial problem-solving: Beginning thought, dealing with, and/or providing explanation about a difficult situation or person to find the correct answer to a question, or the explanation for something that is difficult to comprehend or considered a predicament.

PHASE 3: METACOGNITIVE PROCESSES

1. Evaluating: To judge or determine the quality of something, as in to assess or appraise its worth.
2. Organizing: A systemization of categorizing things, whether this is being objects, thoughts, or feelings. This is to make into a whole part with unified and coherent relationships or to arrange things in an orderly fashion.
3. Critiquing: Thoughts, judgments, or accounting as to whether something is favorable, unfavorable, has both of these components, or resides in-between these. A level of degree is applied to critiquing. Analysis, examination, review, and appraisal are part of critiquing.

4. Collaborating: To work together with another person or groups in order to achieve or produce something. This is done in a cooperative manner, as to team up and/or pool resources.
5. Tolerating: To abide, endure, or put up with by accepting it.
6. Advanced deciding: Reaching a high degree or level of difficulty by providing choice, judgment, explanation, and/or resolution to a situation.
7. Risk-taking: Action requiring grabbing a chance without knowing the outcome of that action.
8. Analyzing: The careful examination of something in order to comprehend it, or to examine the thought and feeling components to ascertain its general composition for comprehension.
9. Synthesizing: To form by bringing together separate arts of a situation in a concise manner, such as to compact its various components.
10. Advanced problem-solving: To find a solution to a problem when there's requirement to do this by there being a "high degree/level" of difficulty concerning one's thinking. This may be by providing explanation about a nonsimplistic situation or person or something that is considered difficult/challenging to comprehend, or explanation for something that is considered comprehensively difficult.
11. Recalling: To bring back to one's mind something from the past as in reference to a memory, whether a moment earlier or a longer expanse of time.
12. Reflecting: To realize something after giving it thought or contemplation by pondering and considering it, as in going back in time to examine a previous circumstance.
13. Self-actuating: Going forward and taking action; doing something as opposed to remaining stationary.

Appendix B

Books with Moral Messages Activity

In chapter 16 of this book, there were directions for an activity involving reading children's literature aloud.

This was first done with a partner and then recording the book title and message of the author on teacher-provided chart paper. The message was what you and your partner thought was an overt/obvious message that the author was trying to convey. Also, what your partner and you thought was the subliminal message/undertone of the book could be recorded on the chart paper. Then, going through the book in an oral reading of what's on the chart or charts, the class shares about the books read. When this is completed the class goes on to separate into partnerships and read another book.

Book Titles and Authors
1. *The Three Questions* by Jon J. Muth
2. *Is There Really a Human Race* by Jamie Lee Curtis
3. *Nobody Knew What to Do* by Becky Ray McCain
4. *If Only I had a Green Nose* by Max Lucado
5. *Today I Feel Silly* by Jamie Lee Curtis
6. *Zero* by Kathryn Otoshi
7. *One* by Kathryn Otoshi
8. *When Everybody Wore a Hat* by William Steig
9. *Don't Laugh at Me* by Steve Seskin and Allen Shamblin
10. *Zen Stories* by Muth
11. *The Kissing Hand* by Audrey Penn
12. *Icky Little Duckling* by Smallman and Warnes
13. *Love You Forever* by Robert Munsch
14. *Words Are Not for Hurting* by Elizabeth Verdick
15. *Pink Bat* by Michael McMillan

16. *The Little Soul and the Sun* by N.D. Walsch
17. *All the World* by Liz Garton Scanlon
18. *The Other Side* by Jacqueline Woodson
19. *When I'm Feeling: Kind, Loved, Angry, Scared, Sad, Lonely, Jealous, Happy* by Trace Moroney
20. *It's Okay to Be Different* by Todd Parr
21. *Yay, You Moving Out, Moving Up, Moving On* by Sandra Boynton
22. *King of the Playground* by Phyllis R. Naylor
23. *Say Something* by Peggy Moss
24. *Bully* by Patricia Polacco
25. *You Are Special* by Max Lucado
26. *What Does Peace Feel Like?* by B. Radunsky
27. *Wherever You Are My Love Will Find You* by Nancy Tillman
28. *Love Your Neighbor: Stories of Values and Virtues* by Arthur Dobrin
29. *Oh, the Places You'll Go!* by Dr. Seuss
30. *I Love You as Much . . .* by Laura Krauss Melmed
31. *Old Turtle and the Broken Truth* by Douglas Wood
32. *Why Am I Different* by Norma Simon
33. *Love My Hair* by Anna Matheson
34. *The I Love You Book* by Todd Parr
35. *Special People Special Ways* by Arlene Maguire
36. *I Like Myself* by Karen Beaumont
37. *The Girl Who Wore Too Much* by Margaret R. MacDonald, with Thai text by Supaporn Vathanaprida
38. *My Brave Year of Firsts: Tries, Sighs, and High Fives* by Jamie Lee Curtis
39. *On the Day You Were Born* by Debra Frasier
40. *Hey, Little Ant* by Hoose and Hoose
41. *I'm Gonna Like Me* by Jamie Lee Curtis
42. *I Can Make a Difference: A Treasury to Inspire Our Children* by M.W. Edelman
43. *What Is Love* by Etan Boritzer
44. *The Next Place* by Warren Hanson
45. *You're All Right* by Joy Wilt
46. *The Lunch Thief* by Anne C. Bromley
47. *Something from Nothing* by Phoebe Gilman
48. *I Hope You Dance* by Mark D. Sanders and Tia Sillers
49. *I Can Do It: How to Use Affirmations to Change Your Life* by Louise L. Hay
50. *The Power of Kindness* by Mac Anderson
51. *Do Not Open This Book!* by Michaela Muntean
52. *The World Is a Gift to You* by Laura Duksta (flip-sided book)
53. *The Way I Feel* by Janan Cain

Appendix C

Character Development Activities: Sequence of Presentation

THE BOOK'S ACTIVITIES

Each chapter of this book has one or two activities in it. These activities, as the author likes to call them, address an interaction between class/course members, a home role-play situation, and workshop or workplace sharing. The sequential order in which these activities appear in this book has been placed in direct conjunction with the chapter topics. In the workshops this author has written and given on character development, teaching for decades at the elementary- and middle-school levels, as well as commencing in 2000 and 2013, respectively: Project SAVE for preventing school violence and the New York State's Dignity for All Student's Act, the following order of activities is preferred:

1. Chapter 1: Scars on the Heart
2. Chapter 2: Getting Acquainted with Sticky Hands Two
3. Chapter 3: Character Development:
    a. Discovering Beliefs and Values,
    b. Knowing about Yourself and Others through Daily Experiences,
    c. Discovering the Differences between Thinking and Feeling
4. Chapter 4: What's Right with *You*
5. Chapter 5: R-E-S-P-E-C-T
6. Chapter 8: A Person of Good Character
7. Chapter 9: Stressors and Causes
8. Chapter 11: Apology Cards
9. Chapter 12: Decision-Making Graphic Organizer

Appendix D

Causes and Possible Prevention of Bullying, Harassment, Discrimination, and Prejudice

(Created by M. S. Schiering 2000, 2003 for Project SAVE)

Behavior: Stress by acting out.

Possible remedy: Be observant and a good listener to those experiencing this stress. Offer support and friendship to self and others. Make suggestions for relaxing exercises.

Behavior: Lack of acceptance by others and self.

Possible remedy: Model *respect* of self and others while practicing, on a continual basis "No put-downs . . . Only lift-ups!"

Behavior: Peer academic rivalry and bias.

Possible remedy: Introduce ideas of not looking alike and therefore not learning the same way (Dunn and Dunn 1978). Address processing styles (Dunn 1996/2015). Discuss origin of bias and "who" one is as an individual. Get to "know" your students and have them "know" each other through social cognition conversations with one another. Using the activities in this book helps to remove the threat of being different, as positivity is emphasized with the "right" of you, similarities in beliefs and values, and so forth.

Behavior: Envy and jealousy of others.

Possible remedy: Examine and realize the good qualities you have. Think and demonstrate: "I am here, I am in charge of me and I am worthwhile." If someone is saying to you that you are not enough or fall short of their expectations, then the problem belongs to that person and not you. Self-talk is to be positive.

Behavior: Feelings of isolation.
Possible remedy: Step forward and communicate with others to create a safe place by building community. Reach out to others you think are trustworthy.

Behavior: Disharmony.
Possible remedy: Institute "codes of conduct" for healthy living.

Behavior: Fear of the unknown.
Possible remedy: When possible, ask questions to make the unknown . . . known. Hypothesize with other on problem-solving (brainstorm) techniques. Avoid retreating into a "dark" place. Communicate *with* others.

Behavior: Loss of sense of security.
Possible remedy: List what makes you feel safe and share this with another or others to see if they may be assistive in relieving the loss. Be willing to change routines.

Behavior: Not belonging.
Possible remedy: Join a group that appeals to you, whether sports, discussion, or an activity that recognizes your input.

Behavior: Fear of failure and those things that bring this sense of not being enough.
Possible remedy: Take action to challenge yourself in such a manner as to achieve success, whether regarding grades or relationships. Listen and communicate with others. Seek out people who are positive in beliefs and values.

Behavior: Rejection and possible indifference.
Possible remedy: Say these words to yourself, "I am enough!" Repeatedly say them to yourself now and continually through this day and days/weeks/months to follow. Come to understand that you are fine as you are. Strive to be the best "you" that you can be.

Behavior: Lack of compassion from others.
Possible remedy: Demonstrate a positive demeanor and be compassionate. Make this an act of your conscious will. While others may not emulate this behavior, you will start to feel better about yourself and realize "you can

only give to another that which you first have for yourself." Teach compassion through your actions so others may see what this is. Many times people copy what's modeled for them so model compassion and the six traits of a person of good character. You can't change another's thinking, but you can guarantee your thinking being positive.

Behavior: Fear of change.
Possible remedy: Try to be flexible and open-minded. Embrace ideas that promote a sense of well-being, even if it requires modifications in your actions.

Behavior: Loss of a loved one.
Possible remedy: Share memories you have of this person. Let him or her be part of "you" in the present.

GENERAL GUIDELINES FOR DAILY LIVING

The following list is from M.S. Schiering (2002) for ideas concerning ways to provide character education and development.

1. "Treat students, teachers, co-workers, family with equal respect;
2. Create ways for students to share their interests, ideas, opinions, concerns, and thoughts;
3. Assist students in feeling safe regarding expressing feelings (sensory responses), fears, anxieties, and emotions (Strong psychological feelings—love);
4. Have a system for reporting discriminating behaviors such as harassment that is overt and subliminal through indifference or ignoring, violence, bullying, cyber-bullying, and prejudice;
5. At every opportunity promote good citizenship and character. Set an example of being a good citizen by practicing the six international traits of a person of good character;
6. Be involved in decision-making instruction and support students making transitions from childhood to adolescence and then to adulthood;
7. Be actively available to yourself and others by being a good listener."

Appendix E

Post-Character Development Workshop: Three Reflections

As explained in the "Book Notation" at the beginning of chapter 1, the contents of this book may be used in a classroom at any grade level, or as a workshop, or in one's workplace or home. While the book is geared to a school setting, it is not exclusive of the others mentioned. You model your character wherever you go and with whomever you interact. At those times you are a teacher of something as much as being the recipient of information through social cognition or, let's say, social interaction.

After a workshop addressing the six international traits of being a person of good character and doing each of twelve activities in this book, this author thought to ask the group about what they thought had been learned, overall. Of course, there is an anonymous evaluation sheet for a workshop, but this request to write after the workshop was conducted yielded the following response examples. These summed up the content of the other responses rather well, and so they are shared here with the name of the person doing the reflection.

REFLECTION 1: NICOLE DeANGELIS

"I very much enjoyed the Scars on the Heart activity. I will be bringing that one to my fourth-grade class. My students struggle with the way they speak to each other and always put each other down. I believe that modeling this "Scars on the Heart" activity will show the impact words have on another and the damage that being negative does.

"I strive to model and set an example for my students, but this singular activity at the start of the workshop was very powerful. I once told my students about my personal experience of being a victim of bullying and they were filled with anger, because it happened to their teacher. They don't realize that I still recall the names of the bullies and impact of these persons had on me so many years later.

"I showed my class that I could still be successful once I faced my bullies and the end result was a powerful moment in my class and we bonded because of our common experiences and talking with each other about them. As a result of this my class now freely approaches me with any problems they have.

"I really enjoyed this workshop. It made me think about all that is said on the topics presented and all that is done as well. For one, I will be sure to keep my sense of humor as well as modeling what was presented today to encourage all lift-ups in our fourth-grade classroom."

REFLECTION 2: ROSALIE RIVERA-CHACON

"The discussions about life lessons in this character development workshop were very clear and full of true-to-life examples that hit their intended point. One of these was that you have to be willing to challenge yourself to have your first success. Another life lesson was "If you have something for yourself, then you can give it to another, but you can't give something you don't have. An example would be caring.

"We did a children's literature read-aloud and then analyzed the story's message. We put our thoughts on a chart to share with the whole class. I liked this activity as it allowed me to see a variety of children's books and get a sense of important themes that I could use to address situations in my classroom. This was a pay-it-forward type of activity that is useful for me and, I think, will help my students."

REFLECTION 3: CECELIA FISHER

"Anyone could benefit from teaching a course like this. We, as humans, need to treat each other better than we're doing now. Everyone needs to be held accountable for their actions and we could all be a bit nicer. Overall, that is what I am coming away with from this workshop. Also, the things that were shared by the instructor—the stories that connected to the activities that were done led me to these realizations."

References

Abbott, J. (1994). *Learning Makes Sense: Recreating Education for a Changing Future*. London: Education 2000.

After, M. (1958). *Stories for My Daughter*. Self-published anecdotes. Rochester, NY.

Angelou, M. (June 2007). *Quote in Village Voice*. Clemmens, NC: PK and Co.

Black, J. (2017). *Decision-making graphic organizer: What if I won a million dollars*. Classroom published presentation for EDU 506A. Molloy College. Rockville Centre, NY.

Bogner, D. (2008/2011). Discussions on Modifications to a Model for Academic and Social. Cognition. Molloy College. Office of the President. Rockville Centre, NY.

————. (2011a). "Narrative on Effective Learners and Teachers: Thinking and Feelings." In *Teaching and Learning: A Model for Academic and Social Cognition*. Lanham, MD: Rowman & Littlefield.

————. (2011b). "The Cognitive Collective." In *Teaching and Learning: A Model for Academic and Social Cognition: and Learning and Teaching Creative Cognition: The Interactive Book Report*. Lanham, MD: Rowman & Littlefield.

————. (2017a). *An Anecdote on Being FAIR* (unpublished). Rockville Centre, NY: Molloy College.

————. (2017b). *Definition of a Good Citizen* (unpublished). Rockville Centre, NY: Molloy College.

Borkowski, J.G. (April 1992/2011). "Metacognitive Theory: A Framework for Teaching Literacy, Writing, and Math Skills." *Journal of Learning Disabilities* 25 (4): 253–57. In *Teaching and Learning: A Model of Academic and Social Cognition*. Lanham, MD: Rowman & Littlefield.

Borkowski, J.G., T.M., Estrada, M., Milstead, and C.A. Hale. (1989). "General Problem-Solving Skills: Relations between Metacognitive and Strategic Processing." *Learning Disability Quarterly* no. 12: 57–70.

Borkum, J. (2017). *An Example of Being Trustworthy: Anecdotes on Civic-Mindedness in Maine*. (unpublished). *Clinical Psychology Practice Journal*. Orono, ME.

Bretherton, J. (1985). "Attachment Theory: Retrospect and Prospect." In J. Bretherton and E. Waters (Eds.), *Growing Points of Attachment Theory and Research*, 32–35. Society for Research in Child Development Monographs 50 (serial number 209). Chicago: University of Chicago Press.

Britzman Mark, and Wes Hanson. (2003). "What Every Educator and Youth Leader Must Know." In *The Case for Character Education and CHARACTER COUNTS!* Josephson Institute of Ethics. Bloomington, IN. Unlimited Publishing.

Byrne, J. (2013). *An Example of Being Caring: My Grandchildren* (unpublished storytelling). Denver, CO.

———. (2017). *Defining Good Citizenship* (unpublished). Denver, CO.

Cino, L. (2017). *Living by Example: Reflections on My Oldest Daughter at Camp. ANCHOR.* (unpublished). Rockville Centre, NY: Molloy College.

Connolly, M. and Giouroukakis, V. (2016). Achieving next generation literacy: Using the test (you think) you hate to help the student you love. ASCD. Alexandria, VA.

Craig, M. (2016). *Thoughts on having classroom harmony. (Unpublished). Molloy College.* Rockville Centre, NY.

DeAngelis, N. (2017). *Reflections Following a Character Development Workshop (Project SAVE).* Rockville Centre, NY: Molloy College.

Dewey, J. (1937). "From Absolutism to Experimentalism." In *Contemporary American Philosophy*, 13–27. New York: Macmillan.

Dunn, R. (1996/2015). "Home Conversations on Addressing Gifted Learners and Processing Styles." In *Learning and Teaching Creative Cognition: The Interactive Book Report*. Lanham, MD: Rowman & Littlefield.

Dunn, R., and K. Dunn. (1978). *Teaching Students through Their Learning Styles: A Practical Approach*. Englewood Cliffs, NJ: Prentice Hall.

Eisner, E. (1997). "Cognition and Representation: A Way to Pursue the American Dream." *Phi Delta Kappan* 78 (5): 349–53.

Elkind, D. (1981/2001). *The Hurried Child: Growing Up Too Fast Too Soon*. Cambridge, MA. Perseus Publishing.

Fisher, C. (2017). *Reflections Following a Character Development Workshop (Project SAVE).* Rockville Centre, NY: Molloy College.

Frost, M. (1973). Understanding My Needs: Need to Belong Series: Basic Human Values. In, The Child's World Inc. Elgin Ill.

Gagné, R.M. (1977). *The Conditions of Learning*. (3rd ed.). New York: Holt, Rinehart & Winston, Inc.

Hanna, M. (2017). *An Example of Being Fair* (unpublished). Nanuet, NY.

Hartman, C. (1987). *Be-Good-to-Yourself Therapy*. St. Meinrad, ID: One Caring Place Abbey Press.

Haugsbakk, G., and Y. Nordkvelle. (2007). "The Rhetoric of ICT and the New Language of Learning: A Critical Analysis of the Use of ICT in the Curricular Field. *European Educational Research Journal* 6 (1): 1–12.

Hayes, B. (2016). *Explaining Character Education*. Course Syllabus: Critical Issues in Education. Division of Education: EDU. 365. Rockville Centre, NY: Molloy College.

———. (2017). *Reflections on Being "Caring" in the 1980s*. Course Syllabus: Foundations of Education. Division of Education: EDU. 329. Rockville Centre, NY: Molloy College.

Kaplan, J.S., and J. Carter. (1995). *Beyond Behavior Modification: A Cognitive-Behavioral Approach to Behavior Management in the School* (3rd ed.). Austin, TX: Pro-Ed Inc.

Kerr, M.M., & C.M. Nelson. (2010). *Strategies for Addressing Behavior Problems in the Classroom* (6th ed.). Boston, MA: Pearson Education, Inc.

King, M.L. Jr. (1947). *The Maroon Tiger.* Student paper. Atlanta, GA: Morehouse College.

Kinpoitner, R. (2017). Thoughts on *What's Right with You: An Interactive Character Development Guide: Foreword (Unpublished).* Molloy College, Rockville Centre, NY.

McGrath, T. (1997). *Stress Therapy.* St. Meinrad, ID: One Caring Place Abbey Press.

Meyers, A. (2017a). "Conversations on the Effect of News Media." In Director of Field Education: Social Work Department. Rockville Centre, NY: Molloy College.

———. (2017b). *Emotional Experiences Shape Us* (unpublished). Director of Field Education: Social Work Department. Rockville Centre, NY: Molloy College.

———. (2017c). *Examples of Good Citizenship: Helping One Another in NYC. Conversations on Good Citizenship for DASA Workshops.* Rockville Centre, NY: Molloy College.

———. (2017d). *Being Enough Explanation for Gift Giving* (unpublished). Director of Field Education: Social Work Department. Rockville Centre, NY: Molloy College.

Miller, N. (2015/2017). An example of good citizenship: Florida's Disney World. (unpublished). Rockville Centre, NY: Molloy College.

Million, J. (1990). *A Rule for Living Well. Psycho-social Drama Webinars.* Florida and Ohio.

———. (2010). *Phone Conversations on Socio-centricity: Wilber's Context in the 2000s.* (unpublished). Rockville Center, NY and Westerville, OH.

———. (2015). *Phone Conversations Regarding Tribalism* (unpublished). Rockville Centre, NY and Westerville, OH.

Moore, M. (2017). *Defining Being Responsible from a Nurse and Mom's Perspective.* Workshop on Responsibilities of a Nurse. Grossmont Hospital. San Diego, CA.

Moroney, R. (2017). *Figure 3.1 graphic design refinement.* (unpublished). Rockville Centre, Molloy College.

New York State Education Department. (2013). *The Dignity for All Students' Act (DASA).* Division of Continuing Education, Rockville Centre, NY: Molloy College.

O'Brien, J. (2016). *Thoughts on the Need for Character Education Instruction.* Division of Education Meeting. Rockville Centre, NY: Molloy College.

O'Connor-Petruso, S.A., M.S. Schiering, B. Hayes, and B. Serrano. (2004). "Pedagogical and Parental Influences in Mathematics Achievement by Gender from Select European Countries from the TIMSS-R Study." *Proceedings of the IRC-2004 TIMSS* 2: 69–84. Paper presented at the International Research Conference, Cyprus.

Panzarino, A. (2015a). *An Example of Being Caring* (unpublished). EDU. 506A: Integrated ELA and Reading. Graduate Course. Rockville Centre, NY: Molloy College.

————. (2015b). *An Example of Being Fair*(unpublished). EDU. 506A: Integrated ELA and Reading. Graduate Course. Rockville Centre, NY: Molloy College.

Rivera-Chacon, R. (2017). *Reflections Following a Character Development Workshop (Project SAVE)*. Rockville Centre, NY: Molloy College.

Rouse, T. (2007/2017). An Example of Trustworthy (unpublished). Philadelphia, PA.

Russo, M. (2015). "Mindfulness: A Summative View." In *Learning and Teaching Creative Cognition: An Interactive Book Report*. Lanham, MD: Rowman and Littlefield.

Russo, M. (2017). Character Counts: Additional Foreword. (Unpublished). Molloy College. Rockville Centre, NY.

Ryley, T. (2007/2017). *A Story about Respect: Character Education and Development*. Tenth-grade English at Baldwin Senior High School. Levittown, NY.

Schiering, J. (2014) *Eradicating Bullying and How to Accept an Apology: Articles for Reading and Discussion*. In DASA (Dignity for All Students Act) Character Education Workshops. Rockville Centre, NY. Molloy College.

Schiering, J., and Schiering, K. (2014). *Three Possible Role-Play Formats for Presentation*. Linx Day Camps, Wellesley and Dover, MA.

Schiering, L., and Schiering, M. (2014). *Examples of Apology Cards*. Linx Camps. Wellesley, MA.

Schiering, M. S. (1967). *Two Types of People: Kind and Unkind*. A fifth-grade slogan. (Self-published) Columbus, OH.

————. (1972). *Feelings Just Are*. Marriage encounter weekend: Self-published as Administrative Couple for Marriage Encounter Weekend Experience. Rochester, NY.

————. (1976). *One Classroom/Life Rule: No Put-Downs . . . Only Lift-Ups!* Poetry by Schiering (self-published) Farley Middle School. Stony Point, NY.

————. (1976–present). *6th Grade Syllabus for DMGO* at Farley Middle School Stony Point, NY and *Integrated ELA and Reading (EDU. 506A) and Interdisciplinary Methods for the Diverse Learner in the Inclusion Classroom (EDU. 504)*. Molloy College, Rockville Centre, NY.

————. (1998). *My Mother's Hands: A Teacher's Reflection:* NORTA News Teachers' Newsletter, North Rockland School District. Stony Point, NY.

————. (1999). *The Effects of Learning-Style Instructional Resources on Fifth-Grade Suburban Students Meta-cognition, Attitudes, Achievement, and Ability to Teach Themselves + The Reciprocal Thinking Phases* (EdD dissertation). St. John's University, New York.

————. (1999–present). *Course Syllabi for Integrated ELA and Reading (EDU. 506A) and Interdisciplinary Methods for the Diverse Learner in the Inclusion Classroom (EDU. 504)*. Molloy College, Rockville Centre, NY.

————. (2000). *The Reciprocal Thinking Phases Identification Chart*. Molloy College, Rockville Centre, NY.

————. (2000–present). *NYS Project SAVE: Safe Schools against Violence in Education*. NYS-mandated program for initial teacher certification. Instructor in Europe, United States, South America. Mainly given for the Division of Continuing Education Rockville Centre campus, Molloy College.

————. (2002). "Pedagogy: A Matter of Sharing One's Experiential Past for Today's Learning." *Academic Exchange Quarterly* 6 (1): 27–31.

————. (2003). "The Cognitive Collective Paradigm: The 'How' and 'Who' of Teaching and Learning." In Raynor et al. (Eds.), *Bridging Theory and Practice*. ELSIN 8th International European Learning Styles Conference. Hull, England: ELSIN.

————. (Winter 2009). "Character Development and the Brain." *Brain World: Humanity's New Frontier Magazine* 2 (1): 28–29, 68–69. New York. IBREA Foundation.

————. (2013-present). The DASA (Dignity for All Students Act) NYS-Mandated Teacher Certification Workshop: Addressing Character Development. Presentations in the United States, Europe and South America. The Division of Continuing Education. Rockville Centre, NY. Primarily given at Rockville Centre campus of Molloy College.

————. (2015). "The Reciprocal Thinking Phases Chart and Definition of Thinking Skills." In *Learning and Teaching Creative Cognition: The Interactive Book Report*. Lanham, MD: Rowman and Littlefield.

————. (2016a). "The Reciprocal Thinking Skills Application to Cognition." In *Teaching Critical and Creative Thinking: An Interactive Workbook*. Lanham, MD: Rowman and Littlefield.

————. (October 2016b). "How to Teach Character Development. CSI Center for Scholastic Inquiry: Research Professional Practice Learning with and from You. Conference. Scottsdale, AZ.

————. (November 2016c). "What's Right with You: Character Development for Everyone: Civility." Circle K International NYS Speaking Convention. Lake George, NY.

Schiering, M.S., and D. Bogner. (2011/2015). The Definitions of Thoughts, Ideas, Opinions, Judgments and Feelings." In *Teaching and Learning: A Model for Academic and Social Cognition. Learning and Teaching Creative Cognition: The Interactive Book Report*. Lanham, MD: Rowman and Littlefield.

Schiering, M.S., D. Bogner, and J. Buli-Holmberg. (2011). *Teaching and Learning: A Model for Academic and Social Cognition*. Lanham, MD: Rowman and Littlefield.

Schiering, S.D. (1999). *A Story about Respect. A Presentation to Doctoral Candidates*. St. John's University. Staten Island, NY.

Schon, D. (1997). "Reflective Practice and Professional Development." ERIC Digest. Retrieved http://eric.ed.gov/.

Spotkov, L. (2016). *A Learning Experience Example: Reflection Realization Lauren S.: Age 22*. Rockville Centre, NY: Molloy College.

————. (2017). *An Example of Caring: An Anecdote*. Project SAVE sharing. Division of Continuing Education. Rockville Centre, NY: Molloy College.

Sullivan, A. (2005–2014). *An Intervention Program When One's Character Needs Improving: A School-wide Incentive*. Thiells Elementary School, 2005–2014. Thiells, NY.

————. (2013). *Reflection on being Responsible: An Anecdote*. (unpublished). Thiells, NY.

Trigwell, K., and Prosser, M. (1997). "Towards an Understanding of Individual Acts of Teaching and Learning: Phenomenographic Perspective." *Higher Education Research and Development* 16 (2): 241–52.

Umanzor, K. (2017). *Caring Is for That Which We Love: An Anecdote.* Freshman Learning Community's Children's Literature: Eng. 262. Rockville Centre, NY. Molloy College.

Walton, A.G. (1896). *The World We Make.* A poem for everyone. http://userxmission.com/~westra/worldwem.htm.

Wenger, E. (1998). *Communities of Practice: Learning, Meaning, and Identity.* Cambridge University Press.

Wilber, K. (2000). *A Theory of Everything: An Integral Vision for Business, Politics, Science, and Spirituality.* Boston: Shambhala Publications.

About the Author

Marjorie S. Schiering, an interfaith chaplain, has devoted her career as a classroom teacher and mother of six to create a comfortable and safe educational environment where students want to learn. In so doing, she addresses the social and academic components of teaching focusing on two basic life statements/in-action rules. These imperatives are: (1)  "No Put-Downs . . . Only Lift-Ups!" (1976) and (2). "I am Enough!" (1990). This author believes that these serve as the underpinning for wherever one is present. For her it was when she was a teacher in Ohio, North Carolina, and Rockland County in New York State, as well as post-graduate professor at St. John's University (doctorate alma mater) and then Molloy College in 1999. She has been at this latter assignment for eighteen years.

Dr. S., as she prefers to be called, carries her philosophy of education with her: "We are all teachers of something . . . be engaged, physically/emotionally/mentally in the learning and teaching process. This interaction will stimulate interest and profoundly assist in retention of information."

Having heard the statements addressing "you are who you are" and "it is what it is" Dr. S. practices teaching the process of discovering how one best learns and realizing that "what it is" . . . is what you decide to do with your personality. Determination and persistence have guided her way in the instruction of self-resolve. Subsequently, she teaches, and has presented internationally on the topics of liking yourself, finding what's right about you, using one's imagination effectively, recognizing and developing creativity, critical thinking, creating classroom communities of learners, how to motivate and inspire the inner you and others, brain-based education with regard to neuroplasticity, and innovative approaches to teaching using her IM (Interactive Method) and learning-through-play technique. "Engage the learner and yourself in subject matter for its optimum retention."

Aside from teaching these aforementioned topics internationally, Dr. S. has conducted the New York State Preventing School Violence (Project SAVE, 2000–present) and Dignity for All Students Act (DASA, 2013–present) workshops for Molloy College each month from September throughout the month of June. These workshops are mandated for initial teacher certification in New York State.

Along with knowing what it is to be a person of good character, as emphasized in these aforementioned workshops, she remains a firm believer in knowing what you're thinking, as it's one thoughts, ideas, opinions, judgments, and feelings that stimulate the way one acts. To that end, Dr. S. developed, in 1999, a Reciprocal Thinking Phases Chart with many cognitive and metacognitive skills identified to assist in one knowing what he or she is thinking.

This chart and its implementation have made it possible to teach thinking and most times do that interactively in courses at Molloy in children's literature for incoming freshmen students, and at the graduate-level interdisciplinary methods and integrated reading and ELA.

Dr. S. is a former first-, third-, fifth-, and sixth-grade classroom teacher, present college professor, processing-style trainer, speaker, author, member of the Oxford Round Table, and advisor to Molloy College's student Circle K International organization. Dr. S. has brought her innovative ways of creative and critical thinking, as well as encouraging use of one's imagination for interactive learning to over 3,000 students in her career as an educator.